Infusionsoft

Table of Contents

I've tried to make everything in this book as accurate and helpful as possible. However, this definitely does not cover all of the possibilities of what the software can do and where things can go wrong. No liability is assumed for losses or damages due to the information provided.

Preface
Introduction

I first heard about Infusionsoft from two of my favorite marketers, Ramit Sethi and Dan Kennedy. Dan has ads for Infusionsoft in his newsletter. I also noticed that when I clicked links from Ramit's emails, I was being redirected to an Infusionsoft URL. I was intrigued, but I didn't really understand what the software did.

I looked into purchasing Infusionsoft, and I realized that Infusionsoft's monthly fee would quickly be recovered by eliminating redundant tasks that I was doing. Plus, I would be able to book more business with the better follow-up and marketing that Infusionsoft would allow me to do.

I took the leap and purchased Infusionsoft. The training and Kickstart that they include is good; however, the strategy behind using the software is not included. There seem to be many users who go through the Kickstart, only to end up with a powerful—but underused—email auto-responder.

Since you picked up this book, I'm guessing that you are in the same position.

In this book, I'm going to take you through what you can do with the software in Part 1. In Part 2, I'm going to help you come up with a plan for your implementation, and in Part 3, I'm going to show you how to use the software.

About This book

This book is meant for beginners. If you've already built one or two larger campaigns on your own, *this book is not for you.*

However, if the only campaigns that you have set up in your account are the ones that were provided by your Kickstart, then this will be the perfect book for you. It will give you the knowledge necessary to get from zero to intermediate user. It will help you understand the functionality of the software so that you don't feel lost when you log in.

You'll be able to use this base knowledge to build the more complicated campaigns that you envisioned when you bought the software.

I want you to build one campaign while going through this book. Having the goal of creating one campaign may not seem like much, but doing so will provide you the ability to understand how the software can work in your business.

Working through this book will reveal the power of Infusionsoft to you. Getting the basics down will give you the foundation to build useful and powerful campaigns in the future.

Don't Worry, This Book Is Meant for Beginners

You probably purchased this book because you are new to the software or thinking of buying it (if you haven't purchased yet, go to http://justinjacques.com/buy for a special offer). As a beginner, you're probably worried because you're not a techie who loves to figure out new software. No need to worry; I'm here to bring you from absolute beginner to having one basic but useful campaign built. Plus, I'll explain how to use all of the important parts of the software.

The good news is that I will make no assumptions about your previous knowledge of Infusionsoft (or that you've even purchased the software)! All the information will be clearly and easily explained.

What's Required to Get the Most of This Book

- A computer (Windows or Mac) where you have internet access and Internet Explorer, Firefox, or Chrome installed to access the internet.

- An Infusionsoft account. Go here if you haven't purchased the software yet for a special offer: http://justinjacques.com/buy

- <u>The most important requirement</u> is that you have the desire and willingness to take the time to follow through with this book, step-by-step.

Thinking of Buying Infusionsoft?

If you're thinking of using Infusionsoft in your business and you're just not sure if it's right for you, go here to sign up for a demo: http://justinjacques.com/buy.

Get the Beginner's Bonus Bundle and Build Your Core Sales Funnel in One Week

I don't want our relationship to start and end with this book. I have a lot more to share with you because I want to help you get the most out of Infusionsoft and truly transform your business. I've put together some extremely valuable resources that I want you to have.

To make this next step entirely risk free to you, I've made a bonus package free for any of the readers of the *Infusionsoft for Beginners*. This free package includes an Infusionsoft Strategy Blueprint, Campaign Visualizer Tool, and Guide to the Best Infusionsoft Add-Ons. To be sure that you don't miss out on the offer, go to http://justinjacques.com/amazing/ right now and accept the offer. It will only take a few minutes, and your journey with Infusionsoft will be much faster and easier.

Get $359 worth of amazing info and tools that will help you plan, implement, and optimize your core sales funnel in seven days...instead of months or years.

...from prospect to lead to one-time buyer **to multi-buyer.**

Remember, amateur marketers make one offer and call it a day when they get a sale. Pro marketers keep making offers. If you're not already doing that, get the bundle to see how you can make it work for your business.

Get it here now >> http://justinjacques.com/amazing/

What You Get in the Beginner's Bonus Bundle:

- My *Core Sales Funnel Blueprint* with step-by-step instructions to the five parts of a core sales funnel that maximizes profit for each lead.

- My *Campaign Visualizer* so you can plan and build your funnel easily without the tech stuff, just a basic mind map of how your sales funnel/processes should go.

- My *Guide to the Nine Best Infusionsoft Add-Ons* to do even more with Infusionsoft like send welcome gifts, direct mail, schedule appointments automatically, and connect your PPC to Infusionsoft seamlessly.

If you want to build your core sales funnel in seven days, you have two options:

1. You can go to this website: http://justinjacques.com/amazing

Part 1: What is Infusionsoft and What Can It Do for You?

Chapter 1: About Infusionsoft

Since I'm trying to take you from absolute beginner to an Infusionsoft intermediate, I want to talk a bit about the software.

What you can do with Infusionsoft is amazing. It can automate many parts of your business.

The problem with Infusionsoft is that many customers are sold on promised results, without realizing that those results will require work and time.

Most customers purchase Infusionsoft thinking that the minute that they are done with the Kickstart, they will be able to kick back and watch the profits roll in.

With Infusionsoft, all you've bought is the right tool. If you leave that tool in the toolbox, you're not going to get results.

Infusionsoft Onboarding (the Kickstart)

I went through the Infusionsoft Kickstart program a few years ago. It has certainly improved since I went through it, but it's difficult to get deep into a software in just a few hours on the phone.

My Success Coach was helpful and definitely taught me a lot about the software. He gave me a good base for how to use it. However, there was hardly any talk about how to optimize it for my business.

A few hours on the phone is not nearly enough for most users to figure out new and complex software like Infusionsoft. It took me many nights of Googling, watching videos, and reading through forums to really optimize Infusionsoft for my business.

That is exactly what this book is meant to help you avoid. I've put all those hours and resources together in one place.

Why I Love Infusionsoft and You Should Too

There is other software out there that can do parts of what Infusionsoft offers very well.

But the reason that I love Infusionsoft is that you get the ability to have your email marketing, shopping cart, and task manager all talking to each other.

With those native connections, you can:

- Send different messages based on whether someone buys or doesn't buy.

- Segment messages based on many other actions like clicking a link, responding to an email, survey answers, or even watching a video.

With this power, you can send sales messages to very specific groups on your list and convert more leads/sell more by talking more directly to each one.

Lastly, building out systems in Infusionsoft gives you the ability to scale. It will take tedious repetitive work off of your plate, giving you more time to grow your business and create systems that make it much easier to bring in new employees.

It gives small businesses the ability to build robust systems that can keep producing profits. It can help you implement systems like those discussed in *The E-Myth* by Michael Gerber, but instead of staff implementing, the software will do the work.

Having these systems in place will allow you to go on vacation and have the business stay on track (and even grow) while you're away. You can also automatically follow up and sell new leads, as well as stay in contact with current clients so that they remember to buy from you the next time it is appropriate.

I hope that I've got you excited about all of the possibilities Infusionsoft brings. It's truly a powerful software!

Now we're going to take one step back. I'm sure your brain is turning with all of the possibilities of what you can build. Stop worrying about all of the possibilities, and let's get one thing done, build one amazing campaign. Let's get a campaign built so that you have the opportunity to see that building campaigns is a repeatable process.

Part 2: How to Avoid Wasting a Ton of Time & Energy on Infusionsoft

"Tactics without strategy is the noise before defeat. Strategy without tactics is the slowest route to victory."
–Sun Tzu

Chapter 2: Plan Before You Build

OK, imagine this. You just bought a plot of land in the mountains. This is going to be your second home, a beautiful place where you and your family will vacation for generations. Imagine right now the great memories that are going to be made there.

But before enjoying this land with your family, you need to build a home. To build your new house, you decide to head to the local hardware store and buy the best tools that they have available. You ask to have them delivered to the lot. You also buy some drywall, lumber, a toilet, some hardwood flooring, and a few doors. Oh yeah, and obviously there will be a roof on the place, so let's get some shingles.

At this point, the helpful hardware employee asks how much of everything you need. You say you hadn't thought of that. He gives you a funny look, and you say, "Just give me what the last guy got." So he puts in the order and you head to the hotel you're staying at, knowing that you have the tools and materials to create the beautiful second home for your family.

You show up to your lot the next day, and the delivery guy asks you where the house is going to be built so that he can drop the materials in the best place. You say you don't know. I'm hoping that at this point, you've realized that you skipped one of the most important steps of building a new home: having a plan.

Without a plan, there will be lots of waste (you definitely bought too much of something and too little of another) and you won't know where to start. Even if you have the skills to use the tools, there will be so much waste that you might run out of time/money/energy before the project is complete.

This is the same story that happens with 98 percent of the business owners who invest in Infusionsoft. They understand the power of the tool and that it can do what they need it to. They have some of the materials that they need to build the system (emails, processes, etc.), but they have no plan for what they want built.

This section of the book is going to take you through the necessary steps of coming up with a plan for your first Infusionsoft campaign.

How Does Infusionsoft Fit into Your Business

In the next chapter, I'm going to take you through how you can plan out a campaign. However, if you're not sure what campaigns you want to build, download my *Lifecycle Marketing Planner* right now. To get it, along with some other amazing free gifts, go to http://justinjacques.com/amazing/.

There are instructions in the planner that will help you plan out the different types of campaigns that you can use in your business.

Chapter 3: How to Painlessly Plan Your Campaign in Two Days

In this chapter, I'm going to go through a process that will help you plan a campaign.

While going through this section, you can work along planning out your Infusionsoft strategy in this book, or you can download the worksheet at http://justinjacques.com/amazing/.

Campaign Goal

Before building a campaign, you must decide what its goal is.

I've heard many users complain that Infusionsoft is confusing. I think the main reason for this complaint is that users don't actually know what they want to do with the software.

So, I want you to pick one goal that you want to achieve with the software and work on only that while you go through the book.

To get started, here are some ideas of things that you can do with a campaign in Infusionsoft:

- Welcome a new customer (with email, phone calls, and direct mail, among other options).

- Deliver a free report that a lead opts in for on your website.

- Send a Happy Birthday email (or even a physical card with ZenDirect—check out my resources to get a full list of recommended add-ons here: http://justinjacques.com/amazing).

- Remind registrants about an event/webinar

- Build a sales pipeline where your leads receive different messages and touch points, depending on where they are in the process.

For now, pick one small task that you want Infusionsoft to do for you and let's build that out.

I'm going to go through an example of a new lead opting in for a lead magnet on our website. Once they have downloaded the report, we will have our sales team call them.

Note: A lead magnet is something that you offer (usually for free) in exchange for contact information. Some examples of lead magnets are Free Reports/Guides, Quizzes, Resource Lists, Free Trials, or Sales Brochures.

Who Is in the Campaign?

Once you have a goal, the next question is: who is into this campaign?

This is important because you would write different messages and build different actions for different groups of people.

Some options of whom you can build a campaign for include:

- clients
- leads
- recent clients
- old clients
- lost clients

You may even want to segment further, so that only leads that have indicated interest in a certain product are in this campaign.

For our example campaign, we are going to have any new leads (coming from our website). These leads will be opting in by giving us their name and email address in exchange for a free guide on "How To Create the Most Profitable Infusionsoft Campaign Ever."

What Starts Your Campaign?

Campaign Goals are what start (and stop) campaigns in Infusionsoft. Goals can be defined by the action that a Contact takes.

To give you a better idea of what I mean by goals, below are some examples.

Your contact:

- signs up for a newsletter
- registers for an event
- attends an event
- requests information
- downloads or views a file
- books a meeting
- calls into your office
- makes a purchase
- watches a video that you've sent
- becomes a client
- tells your sales rep that they want to buy
- tells your sales rep that they are not ready to buy (and gives an objection)

Note: you can have more than one way for your contacts to get into a campaign. For example, you might want someone who calls in to go through the same campaign as someone who fills out your "contact us" form on your website.

In this example, a lead filling out a form on my website (requesting the lead magnet) is going to be the Goal that starts our campaign.

What Do You Want to Happen When a Goal Is Achieved?

What is the first thing that will happen when someone gets into this process? This will be the first step in the campaign.

Some options include:

- they get an email

- a digital product or report is delivered to them

- they get a phone call from a member of your team

- they receive a direct mail piece

- they receive an SMS message

- they receive an email asking them to watch a video

- they're redirected to a survey page

- you direct them to a sales page

- you send them a voice broadcast

In our example, the first thing that is going to happen is that our contact is going to get the lead magnet delivered to them via email.

What Happens Next?

When planning sequences in Infusionsoft, you want to try to think of all of the possible outcomes for that sequence. With most sequences, there is more than one result of that action. Below are some potential outcomes to think about while you're building campaigns.

For sales campaigns, a contact could:

- buy

- not buy

- ask a question

- buy, but cancel

For report delivery campaigns, a contact could:

- download the report

- not download the report

- ask a question

In our example, we are delivering a free electronic report to potential leads via email. The main two results of us sending that email are:

1. The lead clicks on the link in the email to download the report

   or

2. They don't click to download the report

Rinse and Repeat

The rest of the campaign is planned by going through the potential results of each step, then figuring out what you want to happen next. This is where the worksheet comes in handy. Using it, you'll be able to easily plan your campaign.
You can get the worksheet (along with some other awesome free stuff) here: http://justinjacques.com/amazing/.

Again, for our example, our lead could:

1. Download the report
2. Not download the report

If our lead downloads the report, we want our sales team to follow up with a call to see if they have any questions about the report (and to try to make a sale) within one week. At this point, we would end the sequence, since we achieved our goal.

However, if our lead does not click to download the report, we want to follow up with a second email in three days reminding them to check out the report.

This is where the process continues:

The lead could download the report from the reminder email or not download it again.

If they download the report, we can follow up with a call in one week (and finish the sequence).

Or

If they don't download the report this time, we might want to send one more email reminder.

I'm going to stop here, but as you can see, this process can just keep going. Generally, you want to stop once you've achieved your goal and possibly move them to another campaign.

Chapter 4: Campaign Best Practices: How to Just Get It Done!

In the words of Dan Kennedy: "Done is better than perfect." This is definitely the case with campaigns in Infusionsoft.

This is especially true when you're first starting out with the software and you haven't learned all of the ins and outs. Don't get too hung up on making campaigns perfect.

For example, you may forget to remove buyers from a follow-up sequence that is asking people to buy. Don't worry; it isn't the end of the world. If a new client replies to an email, confused about why they're getting a reminder to buy after they've bought, it's not the end of the world. All you have to do is apologize to that person, tell them that something was accidentally overlooked, and fix the problem.

When I first started using Infusionsoft, this happened to me, and that explanation was more than OK for all of the people who somehow got the wrong messages.

It's like using Eric Ries's Lean Startup Methodology: build something that takes a minimal effort that works, then improve on it based on feedback that you receive. This method is going to be the most efficient way to get the best results.

If you don't take this approach, it's going to take you months to get your first campaign launched because you're going to be so worried about making a mistake.

Follow-Up Sales Emails

I always get asked how many times you should follow up with someone in Infusionsoft. You should always send at least three messages about an important action that you want someone to take. That doesn't mean that you keep sending them the same email over and over—it means that you ask for the same or a similar action in three (or more) different ways.

I suggest following up at least six times for really important asks (like getting a lead on a sales call). If you're planning on sending six follow-up emails, you should space out your emails over a longer period.

Meeting, Event, and Appointment Reminders

One of the things that I love most about Infusionsoft is the ability it has to send out reminders. The reason that I love reminders is that they're so simple to implement but they can have powerful results.

Sending out reminders for things like meetings, seminars, webinars, and requests for information from clients (during the onboarding process) is usually a very quick win. Setting up reminders like this takes just a few minutes and results in higher attendance and less wasted time. You can't sell to them or make money if they don't attend.

For reminders, I always like to send one the day before and one on the morning of. If it is a webinar, I also like to include one last reminder about ten minutes before the webinar starts.

I have used text message reminders for certain campaigns. Unfortunately, text messaging is not something that Infusionsoft can do natively, but there are many third-party apps that can be used to add text message functionality to your Infusionsoft install.

If you're interested in learning more about adding SMS to your Infusionsoft install, go here: http://justinjacques.com/amazing/.

How to Write Emails That Sell

I think I could write at least ten books on writing messages that sell. Since there is not enough time to do that here, I'll redirect you to Dan Kennedy's *Ultimate Sales Letter*. This book is one of the best and easiest to follow books on copywriting for small business.

I will include a few important notes about writing messages for those who don't want to check out Dan's book:

1. The message must be engaging. You could have an amazing offer at the best price in the world, but if no one is reading your emails, you're not going to make sales.

2. Always keep your prospect or client in mind when writing emails. Write emails that are useful or interesting to them.

3. Quality is so much more important than quantity. Sending out emails just for the sake of sending emails is a bad idea. Doing so will train your leads and clients to not open your emails.

4. Make sure to promote regularly (but not necessarily in every email). People may stay on your list for months or years. They may not be ready to buy until the fifth, ninth, or twentieth email. Make sure that your emails have regular calls to action.

Part 3: Put your Plan into Action: Step-By-Step Instructions on How to Use Infusionsoft

Chapter 5: Getting Started in Infusionsoft

You've got a plan. Now let's get a campaign built. The campaign builder is the backbone of Infusionsoft, and if you know how to use it, it is truly where the power of Infusionsoft lies. I'll take you through Campaign Builder in the next chapter, but first I'll show you how to get started with Infusionsoft.

How to Sign In

1. Open up an internet browser. Infusionsoft works with Internet Explorer, Google Chrome, and Firefox. Unfortunately, you cannot use Safari (if you're on a Mac). If that is the only internet browser that you have on your Mac, go here to install Firefox (which is my favorite browser): https://www.mozilla.org/en-US/firefox/new/

2. Type https://signin.infusionsoft.com/login into the URL box of your browser and hit enter. The Infusionsoft login screen will come up and look like this:

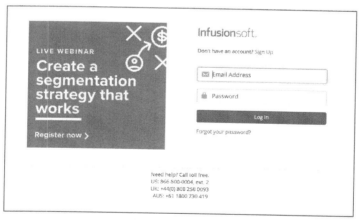

3. Enter the email address that you signed up for Infusionsoft with in the top bar and your password below.

How to Recover Your Password

1. If you've lost your password, click the "Forgot your password?" link that is located right below the Log In button. This will bring you to this screen where you can put in your email address:

2. Put your email address into the box and hit next. When you hit next, the page will look like this:

3. Infusionsoft will email you a recovery code that you can use to login. That email will look like this:

4. You can either click the big Reset Your Password button or put the recovery code into the box on the page that you had requested the reset on.

5. Once you've put in the recovery code or clicked the Reset Your Password button, this page will come up, where you will create a new password:

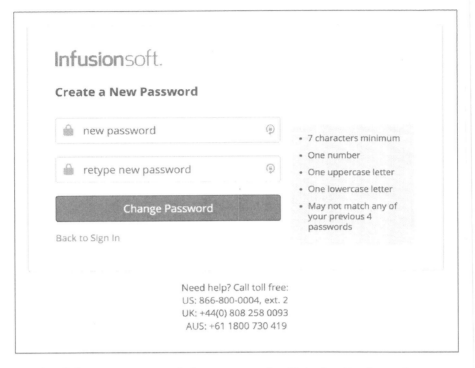

6. Select a password that meets the listed criteria and you now should be able to login with your new password.

One quick tip about passwords: Infusionsoft requires that you update your password every ninety days. Many people find this forced security to be a pain. To make this easier (and more secure), I use an amazing software called LastPass. It automatically generates secure, complex passwords and then autofills them for each website.

There's a free plan with LastPass that is great for individuals. The paid plan allows you to have a company account where you can share groups of passwords with your staff (securely instead of on a spreadsheet).

I highly recommend LastPass to all of my clients. You can get a list of all of my favorite software and Infusionsoft Add-ons by going here: http://justinjacques.com/amazing/.

The First Time You Log In

The very first time you log in to your account, you will be taken through an initial setup. This will ask you a few questions including setting up your email signature, connecting your social media accounts, and adding users.

NOTE: If you have already gone through your basic setup, you can skip ahead to the Navigating Infusionsoft section.

Setting Up Your Email Signature

The new default signature (updated for 2017) is automatically generated from the information in your user profile.

To add/change the information appearing in your signature, go to your user profile by clicking the icon in the top left corner:

Next, select your name from the list of users (you may be the only one at this point).

Your user profile will look like this:

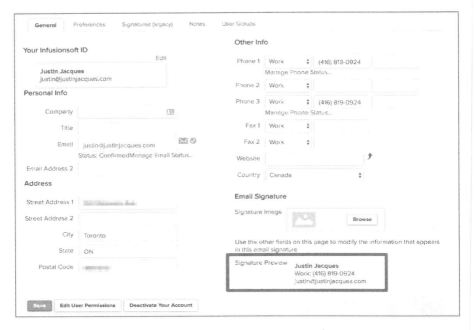

You can see the signature preview in the bottom right corner.

Updating the information in the profile and hitting Save will automatically update the signature.

Notice that, right above the Signature Preview, you can upload an image of yourself, which will show up on the left side of the signature.

Linking Your Social Media Accounts

Next, Infusionsoft asks you to link your social media accounts. Generally I don't think that this is very useful, and it can be skipped.

The functionality that it offers is to post your emails to your Twitter and Facebook accounts. Since Facebook and Twitter are different mediums than email, the messages you post on them and the way you write should be different.

However, if you want to connect your Facebook and Twitter accounts, here's how to do it:

Facebook

1.   Hit the link button.

2.   Log in to your Facebook account.

3.   Once you log in, you will be given the option to connect your Infusionsoft account to your Facebook account; hit okay.

4.   Facebook will then ask you to authorize some permissions. If you agree with the permission question, then hit okay.

5.   Once you've agreed, your Infusionsoft account and Facebook account will now be connected.

Twitter

1. Click the Link button; you will be brought to this page:

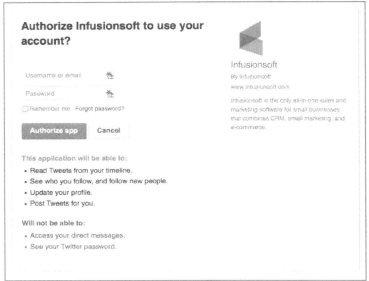

2. Log in to your Twitter account on that page and hit "authorize app."

3. The page will reload; hit "authorize app" again.

4. Your Twitter Account is now connected.

Add Users

You can now add additional users to your application. This is useful for including employees who are going to need access to your application.

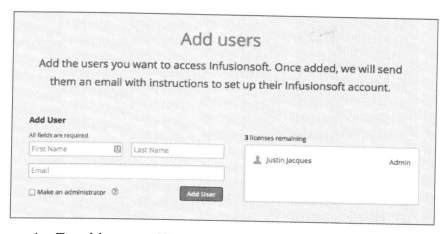

1. To add a user, fill in their first name, last name, and email address.

2. Decide if you want that user to be an administrator.

   Making a user an administrator will give that user unrestricted access to your installation. You can change a user's permission in the future, so if you are worried about giving someone too much access, just add them as a user for now, and you can increase what they have access to later on.

Basic Training

Once you are done with the initial setup, Infusionsoft will allow you to go to their basic training.

The options that you are given are

1. Get Started

2. Manage Contacts

3. Send Emails

4. Automate Marketing

5. Sell Online

6. Manage Tasks

These trainings are helpful, as they walk you through some of the important parts of the software. The problem with them is that they are very generic and don't actually show you how to complete a campaign (the most powerful part of the software). Feel free to go through these at your leisure, but I would recommend creating a campaign by going through the section below and then going back to the training to learn supplemental information.

In the upper right-hand corner of the Infusionsoft Basic Training page, you can click the **Dismiss Basic Training** link. Doing this will move you to your dashboard.

Navigating Infusionsoft's Main Page

When you first log in, this is what you will see:

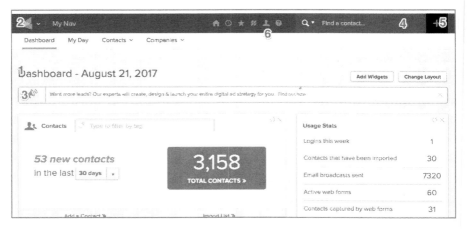

1. The main section of the page is called the Dashboard.

2. The top left arrow next to My Nav is where you find your main menu.

3. These are messages from Infusionsoft. As you can see, on the day I took this screenshot, they were offering help with digital marketing.

4. In the top right of the page, there is a search box for contacts. You can search for any of your contacts here, once they have been imported.

5. Just to the right of number 4 is where you can quickly add a contact, by clicking on the + button

6. To the left of the search bar is the question mark, which is the help button. Click this to begin a live chat during their regular business hours.

My Nav

My Nav (number 2 above) is where you are going to do most of your work. Click this button and this is what you will see:

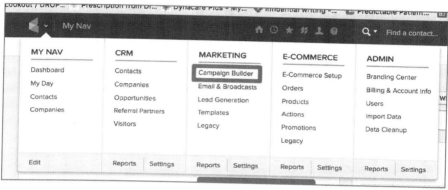

Note: The screenshot above is from an account that has the Complete package, currently priced at $299/month. If you do not have the complete package, you will not have all of the options that are shown above. That is okay, because everything that is discussed in depth in this book is available in the Essentials package.

From My Nav, you can get to the Campaign Builder, which is what we'll discuss in the next section.

Chapter 6: Understanding the Core of Infusionsoft: Campaign Builder

What Is the Campaign Builder?

Campaigns are the core functionality of Infusionsoft. Don't worry about anything else in Infusionsoft until you have a basic understanding of the Campaign builder.

One of the most powerful campaigns, and the one that I suggest my clients build first when we start working together, is a follow-up campaign for someone who has indicated that they are interested in your product or services.

This is powerful because most businesses don't have a good system in place to follow up with hot leads. Implementing a system for this will have a very quick and profitable return.

Get Campaign Templates

Clicking the button below will allow you to start with a base campaign that either Infusionsoft or other consultants have already built out.

Using these templates for some of the campaigns can make working in Infusionsoft faster and easier.

There are currently over 180 prebuilt campaigns. Some of them are quite useful. I find that most of my clients have an idea of what they want to do with Infusionsoft (IS), and many times there are templates that will give them a base to build on and customize.

With a bit of copyediting and some small tweaks, you can use these templates to create very effective campaigns in a very short period of time.

Elements of Campaign Builder

When you go into campaign builder, the first thing you are going to do is hit the "Create a Campaign" button.

You will then be brought into campaign builder and asked to name your campaign.

For now, you can just call it New Lead Capture and Nurture. You can change it in the future, so don't get hung up on the name.

This is what Campaign Builder looks like when you first log in and you've named your campaign:

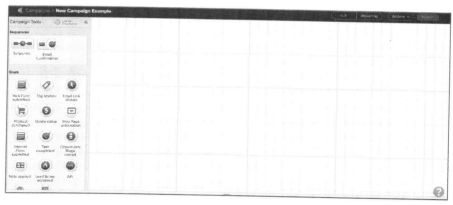

You have a blank worksheet with a toolbar on the left side that has all the potential actions you can add to your campaign.

At the top left, you have the option to go back to the list of campaigns by clicking on the word Campaigns.

Element 1: Actions Dropdown Menu

Next is the Actions dropdown.

When you click it, you will see the following menu:

Here are the functions of the different menu options:

Create a Dashboard Widget

This will take goals in your campaign (e.g., buys, clicks a link, applies a tag) and create a widget (box) for that goal on your dashboard so you can track it.

The image below is an example of a dashboard widget for a particular campaign.

Save a Version

This saves the campaign in its current state so that it can be recovered in the future. Note: Infusionsoft automatically saves any changes that you make to a campaign, but you will not be able to go back to those changes if you do not use the Save a Version option.

Restore Version

This allows you to make the campaign revert back to any saved version of that campaign that you have. I always suggest that you save your current version of a campaign before you restore a previous version. If you don't save the current version, any changes that you've made will be lost.

Make a Copy

This will create an exact copy of the campaign so that you can use elements of the campaign in a new campaign. This is a great way to speed up your campaign-building process.

Revert Changes

Using Revert Changes will undo any changes to the campaign that you have made during your current session only, meaning since you logged into that campaign and began working.

Print

Clicking Print will send a printable version of your campaign to your printer.

Save as Image

This will save your campaign as a .jpg image.

Merge Fields

This is an advanced feature that beginners do not need to use.

Links

This is an advanced feature that beginners do not need to use.

Add a Category

This allows you to group your campaigns into categories so you can find them easier or distinguish between similar campaign names.

Element 2: Publish Button

The publish button is extremely important in campaign builder. You can build the best campaign ever, but if you never publish it, nothing is going to happen. It sounds obvious, but I've had clients forget to publish new or revised campaigns and ask me why they aren't working.

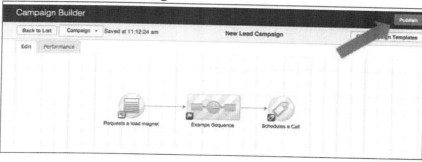

Important Note on Publishing

The color of the icon in campaign builder will let you know if that action is published or not. Unfortunately, this book is black and white, so I can't show you the colors of the icons—but I will describe them to you.

A grey icon in campaign builder means that that element is still in draft mode and is not ready to be published.

There is a Draft/Ready button inside each element (emails, sequences, voice broadcasts, fax letter, internal, and web forms) at the top right corner (see image below). For any element to be published and working, that button needs to be turned to ready.

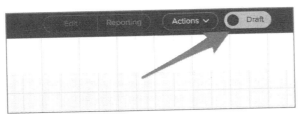

When an element is set to draft, it will not be published, even if you hit the publish button.

If you have something that is ready to be published, you must switch the draft button to Ready. Once that button has been switched to Ready, the icon will change from grey to light green. The light green color means that it is ready to be published **but has not been published yet.**

Once everything you want to publish is light green, you can hit the Publish button in the top right corner of your main screen.

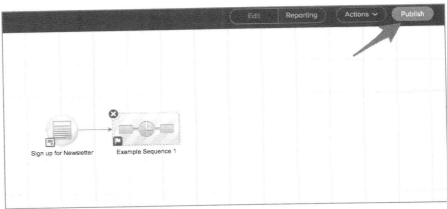

When you hit publish, Infusionsoft will pop up a small window that shows the changes to the campaign. I highly suggest reviewing this before you confirm that you are ready to publish.

Once you have confirmed that you are ready to publish, the light green icons will now be dark green, meaning they're currently published.

Element 3: The Canvas

The canvas is the big white space where you build your campaign.
Important Note:

The canvas does not have a scroll function built into it. The good news is that there are a couple of tricks that you can use to move around the canvas.

Zoom: To zoom in on a Mac, hit Command and +, or on Windows, hit control and +.

To zoom out, on a Mac it is command and −, and in Windows, it's control and −.

To move the canvas, right click (or two finger click on a Mac) and hold and move your cursor. Or hold the shift key and left click and hold with your mouse and move your cursor. This will move the canvas around.

Edit vs. Reporting Screens

If you go into a campaign that is already published, the reporting view will be loaded instead of the edit tab. If you load the campaign and you don't see the toolbar on the left, you know that you are in the performance section of campaign builder and you should click the edit tab (see below).

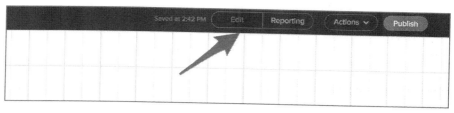

Element 4: Reporting Button

Active View vs. Historical View

The Performance Tab will show you how many contacts are currently in your campaign.

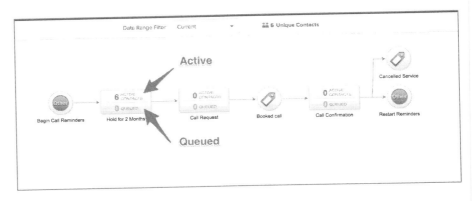

Active Contacts

The big blue numbers on the top of the sequence shows you how many contacts are currently active in that sequence.

If you hover your cursor over the sequence box, you will see a small circle in the top right of the icon come up. You can click on that circle to see the contacts that are currently going through that sequence. These contacts are called the Active contacts.

Queued Contacts

The small gold number indicates the amount of contacts that have gone through the full sequence but have not been moved out of that sequence because they did not achieve one of the goals that follows that sequence and would pull them out (e.g., they didn't buy, sign-up for a call, etc.). These contacts are called the Queued contacts.

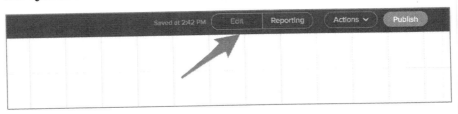

Element 5: Edit Button

Now that we've reviewed what's visible in the Performance tab, I'll go through the edit tab. You need to click on the edit tab to be able to build and edit your campaigns.

38

Element 6: The Campaign Toolbar

The Campaign Toolbar is where you find the different actions that you will need to build a campaign. I will review how to use all of these in the next chapter.

Chapter 7: How to Use the Campaign Toolbar to Create your First Campaign

Below is your campaign toolbar. The Sequences and Goals are the two most important parts of campaigns.

Goals are the elements that start and end sequences. All of the goals can be seen below:

Understanding these goals is very important, so I'm going to go through how each option works below.

Contact Goal: Web Form Submitted

This goal is for when you want to use a form on a website/landing page that leads or clients will submit information through. It's great for:

- A "contact us" form on your website

- Collecting info in exchange for a lead magnet/white paper

- Collecting information in a survey

Once you've dragged the Web Form Submitted form onto your canvas builder, double-click on the icon to edit the form.

This is the screen that will open up:

From here you can add fields and design/format your form. To add or edit the fields that are on the form, click on the Field Snippets tab. Doing so will bring up these options: Name, Email, Other, Radio, Phone, Checkbox, Address, Captcha, Hidden, and Partner.

The Name, Email, Phone, Radio Buttons, etc. icons can then be dragged onto the form and added as fields. If you want to add custom fields to the form, those can be added by using the "Other" icon. Once you have dragged the other icon onto the form, a menu will pop up that looks like this:

You can then select the custom field that you want to use on this form in the dropdown menu Which Field.

The required button (below the Label field) allows you to force anyone who fills out that form to input a value into that field. If you have a field marked as required and a contact does not input a value, they will receive an error message and it will not allow them to complete the form.

One quick note about custom fields is that you only get one hundred of them in your app.

If you're just getting started, that might seem like a lot.

However, I've seen many clients reach this limit, and it's usually because they are using custom fields for adding random notes onto a contact record. This is not the best way to do this.

Instead, you can use a feature called Append to Person Notes.

To do this, drag the "Other" icon onto your form and click on the Which Field dropdown menu.

You will see an option to "Append to person notes" toward the bottom, shown below. That will create a text box that you can write info in and have it be added into that person's notes file.

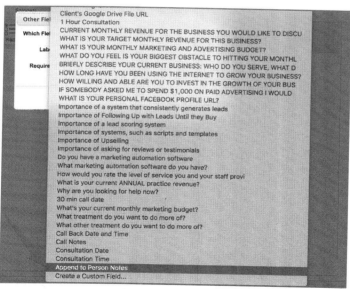

Using Custom Fields

Generally, you should be using custom fields for two reasons:

1. To gather data that you could potentially use in communications with your client. For example, you would want to set up a custom field for meeting dates so that you can send reminders based on that date. You could also use it to collect info specific to your industry; for instance, a wedding DJ would want you to input their client's wedding date and wedding venue.

2. To segment your list. For example, if you're in the weight loss industry, you could send a survey to your prospects asking how much weight that person wanted to lose.

   You would want the answers to be in a custom field so that you could take different actions based on their answers. You probably want to send different messages to someone who wants to lose 50lbs vs. 5 lbs.

However, if you're just looking for general, long form answers to questions, you should be using the Append to Person Notes option.

Setting up Webform Fields

Find the type of field that you want to add to the form. For example, let's use the phone icon. Click (and hold) on that icon and drag it onto the form.

When you have the field snippet in the right spot on the form, a dashed line will show where that field can be placed.

Let go of that field snippet to place that field in that location of the form. Once you've placed the field, a box giving you additional options will come up.

In this box, you'll be able to change the field name that shows up on the form. You can also select whether or not that field is required. Here's an example of what the phone field option would look like.

You can change the text in the checked-off Phone 1 field to have the form show whatever text you want. Since this will be the primary phone number for your contact's account, you can have them write whatever is appropriate for your business.

For example, if you have a B2B business, you might want their office number. If you have a B2C business, you might want their cell.

Editing the Thank-You Page

While editing the web form, you can also edit your thank-you page by selecting the Thank-You Page tab in the top left corner. Here is what the default thank-you page looks like.

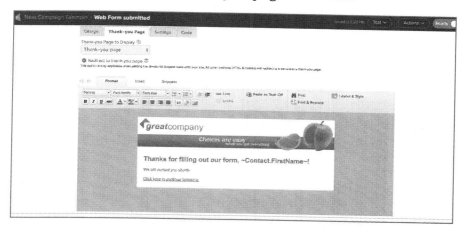

If you select the Settings tab in the top left corner, you're able to change a few settings for the form.

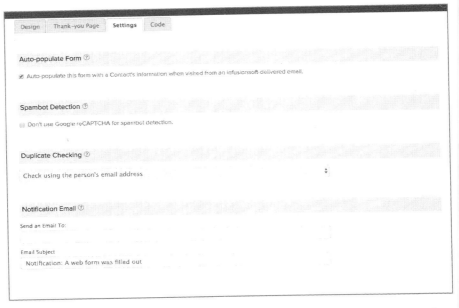

1. Auto-populate the form. This will give your customers the ability to automatically have their email address included in the form if the form is delivered via email. I always have this on if I'm using a form.

2. Duplicate checking allows you to check for duplicate contact records in your Infusionsoft app. You can check based on the person's email address or the person's first or last name. There are additional options that you can see below.

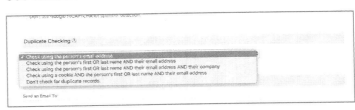

3. You can also send a notification email to yourself or a team member if somebody fills out this web form. This is

an easy way to get notifications if the people filling out this form are hot leads.

Use the Code tab to get links or the code to the form:

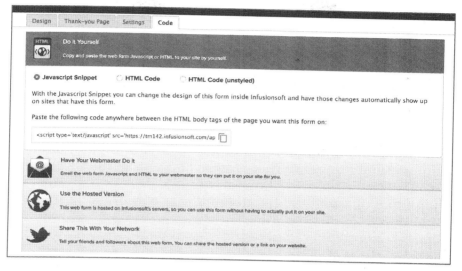

To use a web form on your website, go to the Code tab and select either the JavaScript snippet, the HTML code, or the HTML code unstyled.

In general, I almost always recommend the HTML code unstyled so that I'm able to make the form look how I want on my site and so I know that it's going to work across all devices.

The JavaScript snippet is great because it automatically updates if you make changes to the form; however, the JavaScript snippet can cause problems on a lot of sites, especially for mobile users. If you're going to use the JavaScript snippet, I would highly recommend testing it with mobile devices before making it live on your site.

On the code page, you're also able to just send an email to your webmaster with the code snippet to add to your site.

If you don't need the form to be on your website, you can also use a hosted version of the form. By doing so, you will be given a URL that has your Infusionsoft ID along with Infusionsoft.com in the URL, and you can just send people to that URL to fill out the web form.

User Goal: Applies a Tag

Applies a Tag is one of the most powerful goals within Infusionsoft. Tags are a way to both move your leads/customers/contact records through your campaigns as well as keep track of actions that they've taken.

If you're using tags, this is menu that will pop up once you've selected the goal:

In the field, you can type in the name of any existing tag and it will automatically start searching for that tag. You can also create a new tag by typing in the name of the new tag, then hitting the Add Tag button.

When you create a new tag, you'll get the option to add it to a Tag Category. It will look like this:

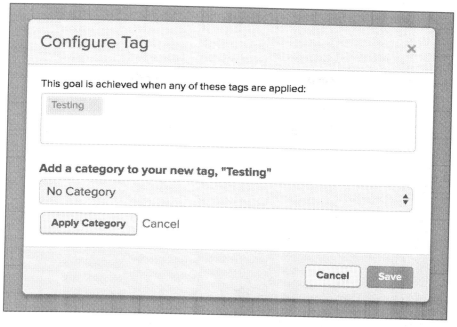

I recommend organizing your tags based on these categories:

1. Trigger—used for when this tag will start/stop and its action.

2. Status—used to indicate the status of a contact; for example, their lead status, Closing, Nurture, etc.

3. Customer—used to mark your current customers.

4. Behavior—used to mark down a behavior that was taken by the contact.

5. Newsletter—used to indicate they're signed up for your newsletter. You can sub newsletter out for any other specific list you want to track, too.

Contact Goal: Email Link Clicked

This Goal is completed when someone clicks a specific link in an email.

This goal is perfect if you want to track when somebody downloads a report, goes to a landing page, or goes to your website.

Note that you can't start a campaign with Email Link Clicked. We'll talk a little bit more about sequences and how this all comes together in the next section. For now, just know that in order for this goal to work, you have to have at least one email in the sequence prior to this goal, like this.

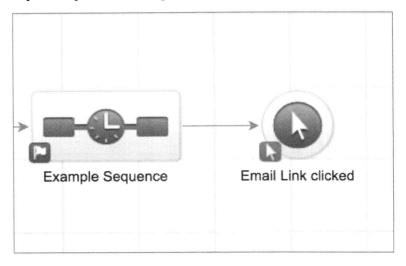

Example Sequence   Email Link clicked

To use this goal, double-click on the icon once it's on your campaign canvas. This screen will come up:

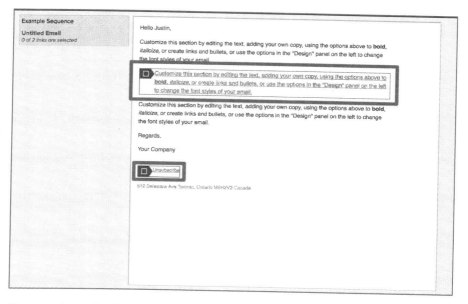

Next, select the link or links you want to track by clicking the check box next to the link.

In this email (shown above), there are two links that can be selected. The first is the link I want to track and the second is the unsubscribe link at the bottom, which we don't want to track.

The first link is for the free download that we are offering. This is the action that we want our prospects to make, so we would check off that link (as shown below).

This goal is great, because if they do not click the link you want, then you can follow up with additional emails until they click one of the links that you want clicked.

By adding this as a goal at the end of the sequence, it will automatically pull people out of the sequence when they click, and they won't get the reminder emails.

Contact Goal: Product Purchased

Product Purchased is only available to users who have the e-commerce or full version of Infusionsoft. This allows you to remove people from a sequence or start them in a new sequence once they make a purchase.

When you use this goal, you can select one of the options: (1) makes any purchase, (2) purchases a specific product, or (3) purchases any product in a specific category.

Doing this allows you to send follow-up campaigns based on a specific product purchase.

You can also tag them based on the specific products that they have purchased or stop follow-up campaigns because they have purchased a product and you don't want to push them to purchase the same product.

Contact Goal: Quote Status

This goal is also only available to those who have the full version of Infusionsoft, and is considered a more advanced feature.

It's used to automate actions when the status of an Infusionsoft quote changes. In order to set this up, you would first have to create a quote.

I will not be covering that in this beginners' book, but you can find out more about using quotes in Infusionsoft here: http://help.infusionsoft.com/userguides/sell-online/create-an-order/create-a-quote/.

Contact Goal: Web Page Automation

This goal is a cool feature, but not something a beginner needs to worry about, which is why I won't go into detail about setting it up and using it.

What it allows you to do is place a pixel on your website or specific webpages, and after someone visits, it can trigger an action.

It's something you can look into doing once you're comfortable with the basic functionality and have set up your main campaigns.

User Goal: Internal Form Submitted

An internal form is similar to a web form, but only you and your staff use it. This is one of the most effective ways to standardize the use of Infusionsoft within your company and ensure proper tagging and movement of leads and clients through your campaigns.

Internal forms are often used to connect offline activity with online, Infusionsoft activity. They can be used to move a lead through a campaign after an action has been completed. For instance, you can use them to mark the outcome of a sales call or consultation.

In order to complete an internal form, you have to be logged into Infusionsoft.

You can access internal forms by searching for a contact by name or email in the search box in the dashboard, then selecting the internal forms button for that contact (shown below):

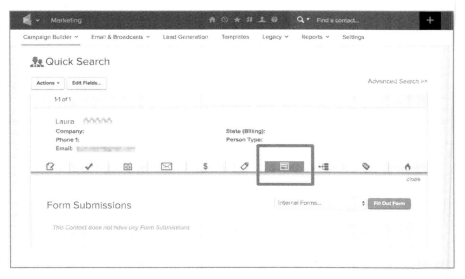

All your internal forms will show up in that dropdown menu. Just select the one you want and click Fill Out Form.

Setting up Internal Forms

The setup and creation of internal forms is very similar to the setup and creation of web forms, but unlike with web forms, you don't need to embed the code on your site because you will be using the internal forms within Infusionsoft.

When you open up the internal form editor, this is what the screen will look like:

As you can see, the default form is set to capture first name and email. To add additional fields, go to the field snippets tab in the top middle/left of the screen.

Just like with the web form, you can add a bunch of different fields to your internal form, including custom fields by selecting the "Other" option.

User Goal: Task Completed

Task Completed is another very powerful goal. In Infusionsoft, you can assign tasks, such as phone calls, to your staff. You can then use the goal of "Completes a Task" to take further action once that task is complete.

For example: You can assign a salesperson a task to call a new prospect.

Once that prospect has been called, your salesperson would mark off that they've completed that task in the My Day area (seen below).

Doing so would move the prospect to the next sequence.

Note: In order to use this goal, the sequence in front of it must contain a task. Once that is set up, you can click on the Task Completed goal and select the task you want marked off in order to pull a contact out of the sequence.

User Goal: Opportunity Stage Moved

Opportunity Stage Moved is a more advanced feature within Infusionsoft. Opportunities are only available if you have the marketing package or the full package.

Opportunities are useful for businesses that have a sales process that requires personal one-on-one sales and manual processes.

Because Opportunities is an advanced feature, I'm not going to go into how to use it within this book.

If you want to learn more about using Opportunities, I suggest that you go here: http://help.infusionsoft.com/userguides/sales-team/create-and-manage-opportunities/.

User Goal: Note Applied

Notes are a way to include information on a contact record about actions that you or your staff have taken.

If you use Note Applied as a goal, here is the menu that will come up:

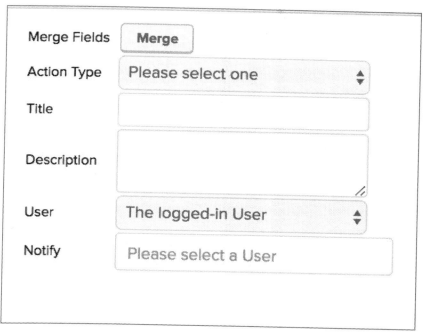

By using this goal, you are creating a note template that will allow you and your staff to quickly register a note on a contact record. Here's how to get it set up.

The Merge Field button just allows you to use merge fields in the Title and Description. For action type, you can choose between call, email, appointment, fax, letter, or other.

You can also add a Title for what the content of the note should be. This will be the headline for the note. An example could be "Called prospect and left voicemail."

The Description section will allow you to create a template for the notes.

Here's an example of how you can use the note templates: I have a client who is a nutrition coach. We use these note templates for her coaching calls. In the Description section, we include all of the questions that she asks her clients, so that she can quickly and easily fill in the notes while on the call.

Next, you can also choose which user(s) that note will be attributed to. The default option is "the logged in user."

Contact Goal: Lead Score Achieved

Lead Score Achieved is a goal that uses lead scoring within Infusionsoft. Lead scoring is a more advanced feature and I'm not going to get into too much detail in this book.

Here's the gist:

- You can give leads a score based on how engaged they are/what actions they take (e.g., if a lead clicks on a link, their score goes up 1 flame). This can tell you how hot a lead is.

- A lead score can be anywhere from zero to five.

- You can automate actions based on reaching a certain lead score.

Again, lead scoring is not a beginner-level feature. I've had many successful clients use Infusionsoft without using lead scores, so don't worry about it until you figure out the basics.

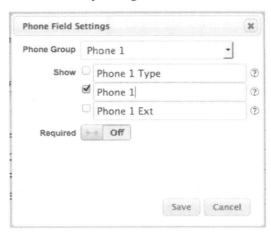

Using the Snippets tab, you can add in other formatting to the form. Using these features, you can include instructions or possibly images or other things that might help ensure that the process is being followed as designed.

I will go through how to use internal forms in a campaign in the upcoming section, Managing Your Contacts in Infusionsoft.

Contact Goal: API

The API goal is not for the average user. The API goal is a way to connect third-party apps to your campaign sequences. Most users can ignore this goal altogether.

Contact Goal: WordPress Opt-In

If you're using a WordPress site, this goal makes it easy to connect forms on your site with your Infusionsoft account.

Using the WP app, you can create forms and pop-ups without any code.

Start by installing and activating the plugin on your WordPress site. Here is what you'll see when you search for it:

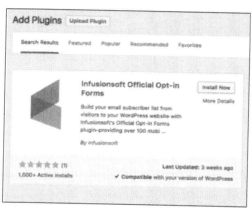

Next, look to your sidebar in the dashboard of WP for the menu item name Infusionsoft. Hover over it and select Settings. Click the New Account button to connect the plugin with your Infusionsoft account.

You'll need to enter the application name and API key.

The application name is the bit that comes immediately before ".infusionsoft.com" in your browser window when using Infusionsoft. For example, if the Infusionsoft URL is tm142.infusionsoft.com, then the correct value to enter in the Application name field is simply "tm142."

The API can be found in your Infusionsoft account by going to your main dropdown menu and then going to Admin >Settings.

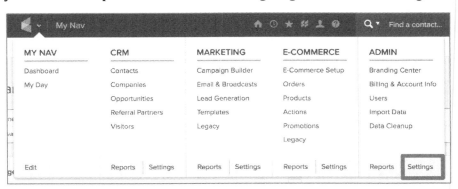

Once there go to the Application link in the left menu:

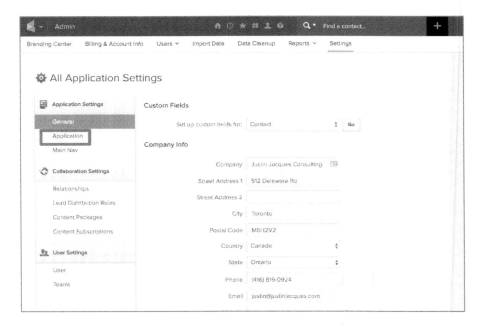

Scroll down to the bottom of that page and copy the text next to the Encrypted Key label (not the API Passphrase, although that seems confusing). Return to WordPress, paste that value into the plugin's API key field, and hit the Authorize button.

If this is the first time you're using the Encrypted Key, you will have to create a new one. Note: You only have to do this the first time. Here's Infusionsoft's instructions on setting it up for the first time: http://help.infusionsoft.com/userguides/get-started/tips-and-tricks/api-key/.

Now that your plugin is set up, you can create your web form.

Under Infusionsoft in your WordPress sidebar, click Opt-In Forms. This will bring you to the Active Opt-In Forms page. If you're doing this for the first time, it should be blank except for a single button. Click the New Opt-In Form button to get started.

On the pop-up that appears (shown below), you'll see the different form types:

- **Pop-Up Opt-In Forms:** Prompt your visitors to opt in without annoying them. You can set Infusionsoft's pop-up opt-in forms to appear automatically after a specific amount of time, after visitors reach a particular point on your page, or even after visitors leave a comment or make a purchase.

- **Slide-In Opt-In Forms:** The slide-in form is the pop-up's smooth, subtle cousin. It slides in at the bottom of your visitor's screen, and can be set to appear after a specific time or at a specific point on the page.

- **Widget Opt-In Forms:** Use widget forms to create attractive opt-in forms for your sidebar, footer, or any other widget-friendly areas on your site.

- **Protected Content Opt-In Forms:** Offering valuable content in exchange for an email address is one of the most effective ways to grow your email list. Protected content forms allow you to offer content your visitors can "unlock" by opting in.

- **Below Content Opt-In Forms:** You can use "Below Content" forms to place an opt-in opportunity at the end of your blog posts or pages. Visitors who have read an entire post are highly engaged, so this is an effective way to turn that engagement into a conversion.

- **Inline Opt-In Forms:** Want to insert an opt-in form in the middle of a blog post, rather than at the end? Inline forms make it easy. You can display these forms virtually anywhere you'd like on any post or page on your website.

- **Notification/Opt-In Bar:** Increase your opt-ins, announce your promotions, and drive traffic to the pages of your choice with an attention-grabbing, top-of-page banner.

In this example, we're going to choose the first one, Pop Up, to create a simple pop-up on your site.

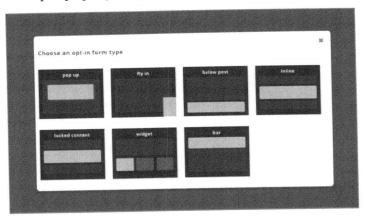

On the next screen, you can name your form. In this case, we'll call it Example Pop-Up Form.

Next click the **Next: Design** to design your pop-up. On this page, you'll see three examples of form layouts. Click one to show a selection of preconfigured designs that use that layout. If you choose one and you decide you don't like the options that appear, you can simply select another layout at the top.

Once you've selected an option you like, click the **Next: Customize** button at the bottom to see all the advanced customization options.

To set up the thank-you option when a person completes the form, you can either select the checkbox that says **Redirect to URL after opt-in** and enter the URL of your thank-you page, or you can leave this box unchecked and simply type a message into the Success Message Text area. This message will display to your visitors after they've submitted the form.

Now onto the last step inside of WordPress. First, click the **Next: Display Settings** button.

There are a lot of options on this page, but I think the important ones are:

- **Trigger After Time Delay and Delay (in seconds)**—can be used together to control how long a visitor is on a page before the form appears (or, if deselected, to prevent it from automatically showing up).

- **Trigger When Element Is Clicked**—makes a shortcode available in the WordPress post/page editor to create a clickable link.

- **Display Once per Session**—displays a second option.

  - **Session Duration (in days)**—lets you restrict how often a visitor will see this pop-up on the same device.

- **Display on and Display on Categories**—lets you select/deselect which types of content this pop-up should appear for. There are also a few other options that let you selectively allow/disallow the pop-up on specific pages or posts.

Once you've customized these options, click Save & Exit and go back into your Infusionsoft campaign.

Once you're in the campaign where you want to use the WordPress Opt-In goal, you can drag your goal onto the campaign canvas and double-click on it.

In the search box that appears, start typing, and the name of the form that you created in WordPress will become available for autocompletion. Select the form (in this case, Example Pop-Up Form) and click Save. Connect your WordPress Opt-In goal to a sequence, and you're ready to use it.

Contact Goal: Submits a Landing Page Form

A Landing Page Form allows you to design and create a full webpage using Infusionsoft's relatively easy to use drag-and-drop editor.

Although you can use the Landing Page Forms, I personally use LeadPages and Unbounce, which are both third-party software.

LeadPages is great because the layout and design of their landing pages are tested and optimized by their user base.

Unbounce gives you more design options than LeadPages; it also uses a drag-and-drop editor, giving you more design and layout flexibility.

Both give you the ability to A/B test your landing page, where that is not native to Infusionsoft's landing page technology.

They also both integrate with Infusionsoft.

You can go to http://justinjacques.com/amazing to get a list of all of the resources and software that I've mentioned in this book.

If you would like to use the landing page technology in Infusionsoft, it will allow you to build a landing page that looks decent and is a good first step to get your lead capture campaign up and running. Plus, you won't have to learn or pay for another tool right now.

When you open up the landing page builder within your campaign builder, this is what it will look like:

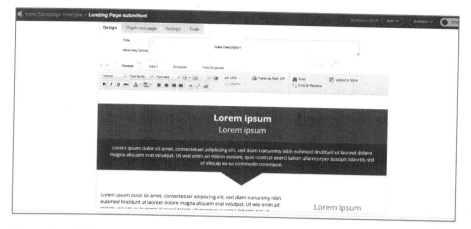

The tab will be set to Design. If you scroll down, the editor will be similar to the email editor, where you're able to change out different parts, including the logo, the different sections of the page, and the information you'll be capturing in the built-in form.

At the top of the landing page design page, you'll see the fields "Meta Key Words" and "Meta Description." These are important if you are using the Infusionsoft-hosted version of the landing page and not copying the code onto your own website.

The Meta Title is the headline that will show up as your website headline in Google, Bing, etc. organic search results.

It will also be displayed in the top of your browser bar. If you're looking at your Firefox/Chrome/Safari/Microsoft Explorer window, you will see words for each tab along with a little icon.

The Meta Keywords are truthfully not important; however, you could put a few keywords in there. Keywords are an outdated and unnecessary part of websites now. Search engines previously used them, but since they were misused by many websites, search engines no longer pay attention to the keywords.

The Meta Description is what will show up below the headline in your organic search results. For example, I've taken a screenshot of Infusionsoft's search result, and you'll see below that the page title is "Infusionsoft: Small Business CRM I Marketing Software..." and the meta description is in the box.

Editing the Thank-You Page

You can edit the thank-you page—the page that leads land on after they submit their info—by clicking on the Thank-You Page tab in the top left corner.

The Settings tab, in the top left corner, offers the same features as the Web Form Settings tab, which I went through on page 46, so I won't review that again here.

The Code tab is where you find the URL of the landing page that you've created.

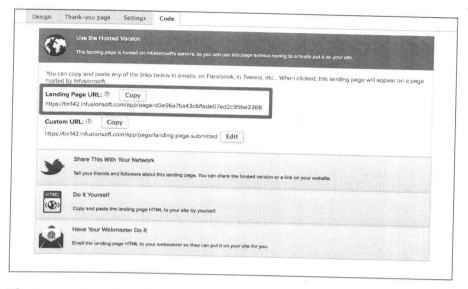

The top option, Landing Page URL and Custom URL, are links that you can send traffic directly to the landing page you just created.

Note that by choosing to use these URLs, the URL of your page will have Infusionsoft.com in it, but this makes it easier because you don't have to implement any code in your site.

If you want to create your own URL, go down to the section "Do-It-Yourself." This will provide HTML code that you can paste into your site.

Infusionsoft for Beginners

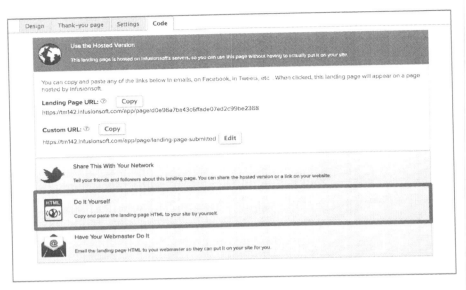

Clicking the two blue squares on the right side (screenshot below) will automatically copy the code so you can just go to the backend of your website and paste it in.

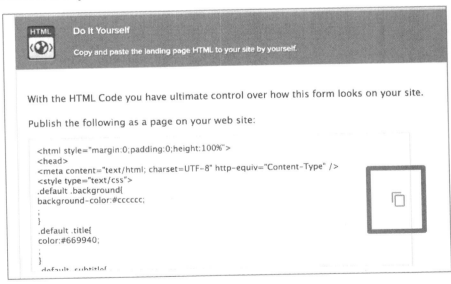

68

Chapter 8: How to Use Campaign Builder Sequences

Sequences are where all of the actions take place in Campaign Builder. Together, goals and sequences are the only two functioning parts of the Campaign Builder.

Using Sequences, you can send email, create tasks, append notes, and add and remove tags from your contact records.

To use a sequence, start by dragging the sequence box from the left menu onto the campaign canvas.

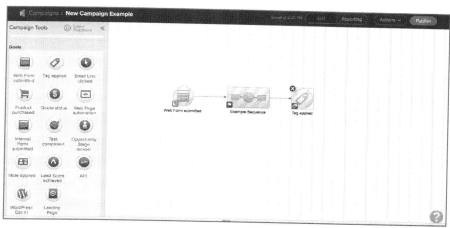

Once you've added a sequence, double-click on the icon and this is what you'll see:

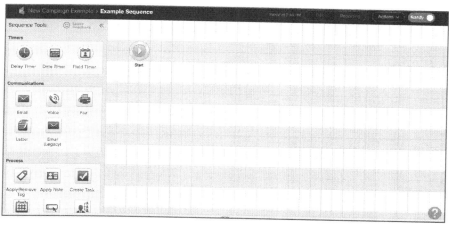

69

In the top left corner, you can click on the campaign name—in this case, "New Campaign Example"—and you'll be able to go back to the campaign canvas.

Sequence Dropdown Menu

On the top right, there's the sequence menu called Actions. If you click on the Sequence menu, you'll see the options

- Rename…

- Print

- Save as image

- Copy from campaign

It looks like this:

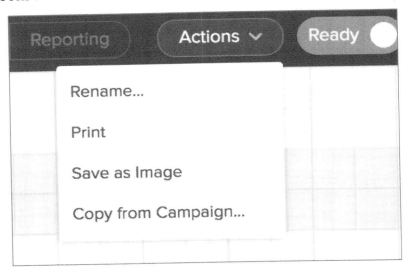

Rename…—allows you to change the name of the sequence.

Print—allows you to print an image of the sequence.

Save as Image—allows you to save an image of the sequence.

Copy from Campaign—allows you to copy a sequence from another campaign. This can be a great way to save time if you're building similar sequences in several campaigns. Note that in order to copy a sequence, it must be published.

In the top right, you'll also see a Draft/Ready toggle switch. This sequence is currently switched to draft mode.

In order to publish a campaign, it has to be switched to Ready. To change a sequence that is in "draft" to "ready," all you have to do is click the button.

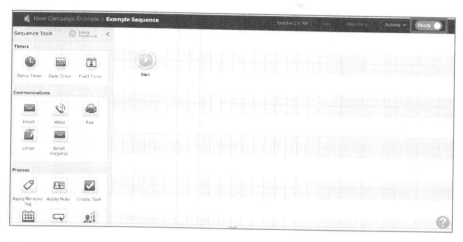

Within the sequence page, there is a toolbar on the left side.

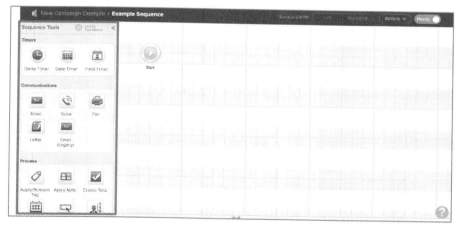

This toolbar has different options than the toolbar on the Campaign Canvas. I will explain each below.

Sequence Tools

Similar to Campaigns, Sequences have their own toolbar.

Timers

Sequence Start Timer

The Start Timer is the only tool that will already be on your sequence canvas (shown below). It belongs at the beginning of all sequences. You can have multiple Start Timers in a sequence.

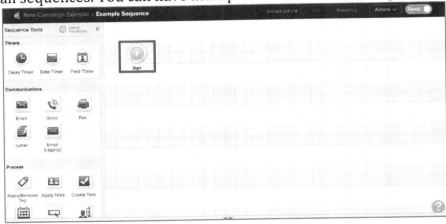

Sequence Delay Timer

The delay timer allows you to set a specific delay period before a contact moves forward in a sequence. It is not based on a calendar date, just a timeframe delay—one minute, one hour, one day, etc. If you want a contact to get an email one day after completing a goal, like completing a form, this is the timer that you should use.

If you use a Delay Timer, this is what the menu looks like:

Menu Options:

Column 1

Wait at least: allows you to choose the delay period before a contact can move on in the sequence. You can set the delay time in minutes, hours, days, weeks, or months.

You can also use the no-delay if you only want sequences to run on certain days of the month or times, which you can select in the next two columns to the right.

Column 2

Run on: you can select any day, week day, weekend, day of the week, or day of the month. You can have actions based on almost any date configuration that you want.

Day of the week allows for multiple selections. This is what will come up if you select it in the dropdown menu:

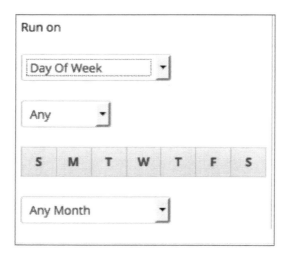

As you can see in the picture above, the S-M-T-W-T-F-S represents Sunday through Saturday. You can select which day of the week you want by clicking on it.

Column 3

At or Between: you can send it at a specific time or between certain times. If you want an email sent at a specific time, you would choose "at." If you want to trigger actions during a certain period of the day, like during your workday, use the between option.

If you use the between option and set the time for 8 AM and 5 PM, the next action would only take place during those hours. If a contact came through this sequence at 6 pm, it would wait until the next morning at 8 am to take the next action step, like sending an email.

Example: If you want to automatically send a certain email on Monday, during business hours, you would:

1. Choose no-delay in the "Wait at least" column.

2. Choose Day of Choice in the "Run On" dropdown menu. Then choose M (for Monday) as the day.

3. Select "Between" in the third column. Then choose 8:00 AM as the first time and 5:00 PM as the second time.

This setup will hold all contacts until Monday at 8 AM. Once Monday hits, the contacts will move forward in the sequence.

If someone goes through the timer at 3 PM on Monday, it would trigger immediately, since we selected for it to run between 8 AM and 5 PM.

Sequence Date Timer

The options for the Date Timer are stricter than those for the Delay Timer. Use this timer if you want to pick a specific date or between specific dates on the calendar. The date includes the year so you can only have it set to send only one time. This is great for setting up a one-time sale or for a special date for your clients. For example, if you were an accountant, you could set the timer to send out a reminder one month before the tax deadline.

The menu for this timer will look like this:

Sequence Field Timer

Field timers are extremely powerful. You can use them to set up actions based on dates from set fields or custom fields, such as birthdays or sign up dates. They are great for appointment reminders as well.

The setup of the Field Timer is similar to the Delay Timer, shown in the menu below:

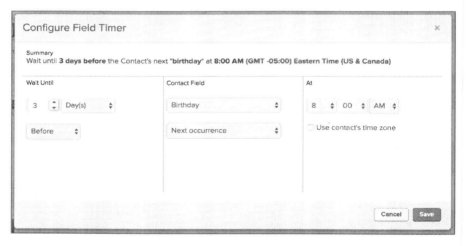

Column 1—Wait Until

In the Field Timer, you can have actions occur before or after the field. If you wanted to send a birthday message, you could set up the timer to send it on somebody's birthday or a day or two before a scheduled appointment to remind them.

Column 2—Contact Field

Choose the date field that you want to create an action around.

Below the Contact Field menu is a dropdown menu with two options—Next Occurrence and Year From Field. Next

Occurrence means that the timer will trigger the next time this date occurs, regardless of the year. Use this option for recurring messages/actions like birthdays or anniversaries.

Year From Field allows you to take action on contact records based on the year in the field chosen above. Use the Year From Field when you only want an action taken in the year from the field, like for an appointment.

For instance, a mortgage broker could use this to send an email reminder six months before a mortgage renewal date.

Using the Timers

To use these timers within a sequence, drag one over onto the Sequence Canvas. Hover over the Start Timer or previous icon, and you should see a green arrow. Click on that green arrow, hold, and drag it over onto the timer icon that you want to connect it to.

Note: You cannot use multiple types of timers in the same chain. For example, you can't use Field timers and Delay timers in the same chain of actions.

If you want to use different timers in the same sequence, start a separate chain below with a new Start icon.

Communications

Email

To use an email within a sequence, click on the email icon and drag it onto your canvas. You will then see a grey email icon on your canvas with Untitled Email below. If you have removed the timers from the previous section, your campaign will look like this.

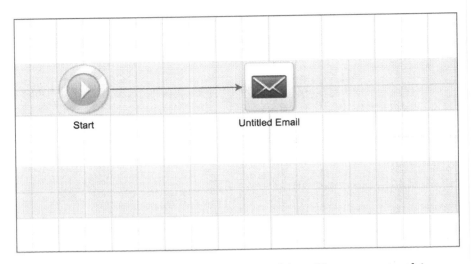

To edit the email, double-click on it and it will open up to this screen:

These are the different email templates you can use. If you want your email to look like a normal email, scroll down to the option that's called Simple Text.

Once you find a template you like, hover over it with your cursor and select Use Template.

Now you're in the email editor, and you can set it up.

At the top left, you can go back to the sequence canvas by clicking the sequence name (shown in the box below).

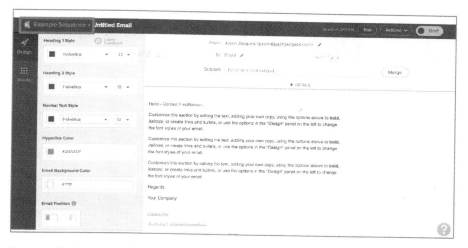

You will also see the name of the email next to the sequence name.

Over on the right side is the dropdown email menu. If you open the email dropdown, this is what it will look like:

Within the email menu, you can

- Preview the email. This will open a preview screen of the email that you are working on.

- Save your email as a template. This will save the email that you are working on into a template so you can reuse it in other emails.

- Rename the email. This will rename the email in the sequence.

To the right of the email menu is Send Test, where you can send a test email to any of the Infusionsoft users you have on your account.

To the right of that is the Draft/Ready toggle button. You can switch this from Draft to Ready when you are done setting up the email.

First, to edit whom the email is coming from and the subject line, go to the top of the email. When this section is collapsed, all you'll see is Details at the top. Click on it to have this section drop down again.

To edit whom the email is being sent from, click on the small pencil next to the email address that appears at the top.

Below that, you're able to set the To option to any email address in your Contact's Record. The default is the Contact's primary email address, shown as Email.

Further below that you can write the subject, which is what will show up in the subject line in your Contact's inbox.

To the right of the subject, you'll see the Merge button. Clicking on this will pop up your options for the merge fields.

To see what this looks like, just look below:

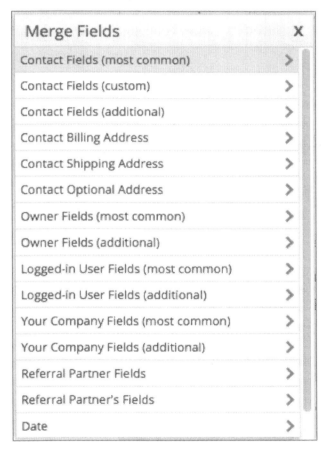

Merge fields allow you to use information from your Contact's Record in an email. A common example of using this is if you want to personalize an email with your contact's first name.

To merge a field into an email:

1. Click on the merge button to open the menu above.

2. Click in the email where you want the field to go. For example, if you wanted to personalize an email with first name data, then in the email write "Hi." Click your cursor to follow the "Hi."

3. Go to the merge menu and click on the "Contact Fields (most common)" button.

4. Click on First Name. This should put ~Contact.FirstName~ into your email where your cursor was.

If you have this, any email that you send will replace ~Contact.FirstName~ with the contact's first name.

You can click through the merge menu to explore all the merge options available.

Formatting your Email

To format your email, first check out the two options on the far right, Blocks and Design.

Blocks is all the different drag-and-drop boxes that you can add to your email. To add a box to your email, just click on it and drag it on. When you hover over the email, you will see a dashed box appear. Drag the snippet to where you want it to appear in the email and let go when the dashed box is where you want the snippet to go.

The block options are:

1. Text

2. Spacer—puts a vertical space between boxes or at the beginning or end of the email. You might use this to move certain elements down on the page, to make the email easier to read.

3. Divider—puts a horizontal dividing line in the email. The weight and color of the line can be adjusted after you drag it onto the email builder.

4. Image

5. Button—can be used to send people to URLs, phone numbers, file downloads, forms, and email addresses.

6. Social—adds the social media icons to your email and allows you to connect your accounts.

7. Group—drops in an image, text box, and button in one block.

8. Video—links to a YouTube video and shows a thumbnail of the video in the email. Note: You cannot play the video in the email, you're just linking to it.

9. Signature—allows you to set the signature to any Infusionsoft user set up in your account. If you want a different signature, then you'll just write it out in a text block.

The second box on the far left, Design, allows you to set the font styles and colors for the three types of text in your email—normal text, Heading 1, and Heading 2.

Note that you cannot add additional styles and must make do with only three at this point.

Here you can also change the Hyperlink Color and Email Background Color.

The last menu you need to know about in the email builder is the Text Menu (shown below).

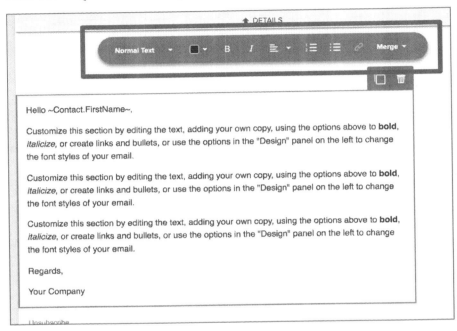

To get this menu to appear, simply click anywhere in the text area of a text box.

This menu will allow you to change the text style, color, alignment, and bullet points/numbering. You can also make the text bold or italicized and hyperlink the text. Note that there is no option to underline text.

You can also click on the Merge dropdown menu to bring up the Merge fields and add them to your email.

If you want to hyperlink text, just highlight it, then click the Link button, and this will pop up:

You can then choose what you want to link to. If you're linking to a website, choose Web Address from the dropdown menu and paste the web address in the bar below. Make sure you test the link in a test email to ensure it works and redirects properly.

The other link options from the dropdown are below:

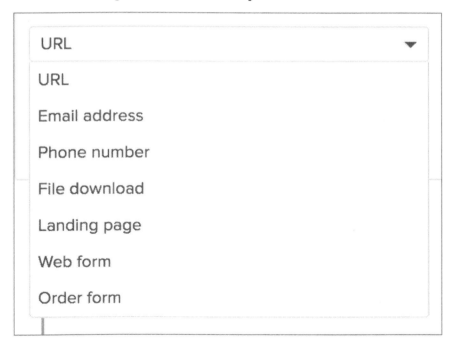

- An email address would be an email address that somebody could click on, causing their email application to open (e.g., Outlook, Gmail).

- <u>A phone number</u> would open up a phone app on their phone or one on their computer if it's set up.

- <u>A file download</u> will allow you link to a file in your Infusionsoft account so that the email receiver can download it when they click on the link. You can select a file that you have already added to Infusionsoft or you can click the Add New File button and upload a file.

- <u>A landing page</u> allows you to link to an Infusionsoft landing in your account.

- <u>Web form</u> allows you to link to a web form in that same campaign. Choosing it will give you a dropdown menu of the web form options.

- <u>Order form</u> allows you to link to order forms in that same campaign, just like the web form option.

Note the Plus Tag button, located next to the Link To option:

Clicking this will allow you to add a tag if somebody clicks on the link that you provided.

This is useful to track actions that your Contact Records have taken.

Once you have written and formatted your email, go to the top right corner and turn the email from Draft to Ready. You can then exit and return to the sequence by clicking the sequence name in the top left corner.

Voice

Voice is an interesting marketing option that allows you to call and play a recorded message to your contacts.
Voice Broadcast costs $0.15/min. and international rates may vary.

Once you have added a voice broadcast to a sequence, double-click on the icon and this is the menu that you will see:

Configuring your Voice Broadcast

The first time you use voice broadcast, you will have to set up your caller ID before you can use the feature. To set up your caller ID, click the top Add Message button.

You will then be prompted to set the phone number for your caller ID, as shown in this menu:

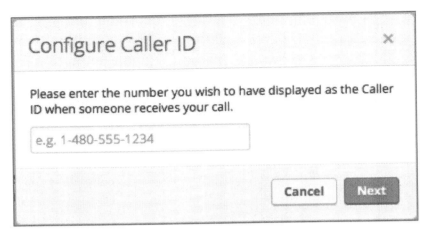

This is the number that will show up on your contact's caller ID.

I usually suggest using your office's main number so that your contacts know who is calling.

Now that you have set up your caller ID, you will be able to add a message.

You can set up your voice broadcast messages to be different based on whether a live person answers or if you get voicemail.

To add a message for if a live person answers your call, click the add message button here:

Once you click the Add Message button, you will be able to record your voice broadcast by having an automated system from Infusionsoft call you. Here is the menu that you will see:

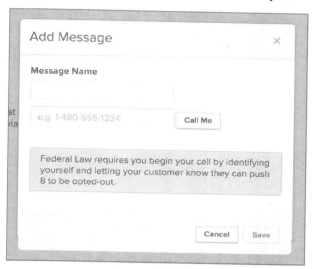

The Message Name is the file name so that you can keep track of each message that you are using. If you were calling your contacts about a T-shirt sale on June 20th, 2018, you might want to name the message "T-shirt sale 06/20/2018."

The next step is to put in the phone number where the automated system can call you and hit the Call Me button. Infusionsoft's automated system will then call you and ask you to hit 1 and record a message.

When you're ready, hit 1 and listen to the instructions.

Once you're done recording the message on the phone, you will be able to select that message on the main Voice Broadcast screen. Click on the "Select a recorded message" dropdown menu and find the name of the message that you just recorded.

You can then repeat the process to record the message for if your voice broadcast reaches a voicemail by clicking this button:

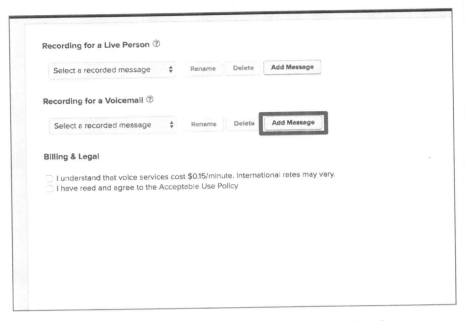

Before switch your Voice Broadcast from Draft to Ready, you must agree to the Billing & Legal terms by checking these boxes:

Billing & Legal

☐ I understand that voice services cost $0.15/minute. International rates may vary.
☐ I have read and agree to the Acceptable Use Policy

Fax

Broadcast fax is an interesting marketing option. Faxes are becoming less common every day. Depending on the industry, it could be easier to stand out by using a fax as compared to email. With email, you're potentially competing with hundreds of emails a day. With fax, many companies may not receive many these days.
It's not guaranteed to work in every industry, but could be worth testing.

When you add a fax to a sequence, this is the menu that you will see:

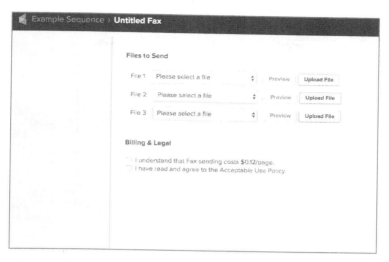

Along the top bar, you will see the usual elements: Sequence Name, Fax Name, the Action Menu, and a Draft/Ready switch.

If you click on the Action dropdown menu, you'll see:

- Rename—allows you to rename the fax.

- Save as a template—saves this fax as a fax template, so that you can easily use it in other campaigns.

- Use template—allows you to use a template you've already created and saved.

- Copy from Campaign—allows you to copy a fax from another campaign, even if you haven't saved it as a template. To do this, you just have to know the name of the campaign and sequence that the fax that you want to copy is in.

All of these options are for saving time.

You can send up to three different files in one fax.

You can use a file that you've already uploaded or you can upload a new file by clicking on one of the Upload File buttons.

Before switch your Fax Broadcast from Draft to Ready, you must agree to the Billing & Legal terms by checking these boxes:

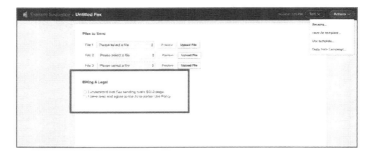

Letter

Unlike Faxes, Emails, or Voice Broadcasts, Letters are not fully automated with Infusionsoft. If you include a Letter in a sequence, one of your users will be assigned the task of sending the letter.

If you want to fully automate direct mail, you can find my recommendations for third-party software that can do that here: http://justinjacques.com/amazing/.

Editing a letter is similar to editing an email. Just refer to the email section if you need more direction on how to edit a letter.

Processes

Apply/Remove tag

Apply/Remove Tag applies tags or removes tags from your Contact Records.

Tags are one of the most useful functions of Infusionsoft.

There are three main reasons for using tags in Infusionsoft:

1. Historical data collection. You can use tags to keep a record of what actions contacts have taken. An example of this is that you can tag your clients based on what products they have purchased.

2. Track status in your sales funnel. This can be as basic as having lead, client, and past client tags. Or it can get more complicated, where you track all the steps of your sales and client cycle.

3. Start and stop sequences for your contacts. Many people call these Trigger tags.

Here's an example of how you would do that. A lead is in a follow-up sequence after downloading a brochure. The follow-up sequence includes three emails and one phone call to try and get them to buy.

If they don't buy by the time they reach the end of the sequence, you could apply a trigger tag that would put the lead into a generic follow-up sequence so you could stay in touch with them.

To set this up, you would add the tag at the end of the follow-up sequence chain. You would also have to put that same tag in front of the next sequence you wanted them to start.

Note: When using tags as goals, the goal will only be achieved when the tag is applied the first time. If a contact already has a tag, the goal will not be achieved when the tag is applied a second time.

The best way to think of Trigger Tags is to imagine them as buttons. Once a Trigger Tag is applied (and the button is pushed), you cannot push it again until it has been reset. To reset the button, you have to remove the tag from the contact record.

Apply Note

The next process that you can use is Apply Note, which applies a note written in this action to the Contact Record. You could apply a tag to note a Contact Record's action instead of a note— for example, "downloaded lead magnet"—but the advantage to using a note is that it will timestamp when the note was added. You can edit the Note to say whatever you want by double-clicking on it. Here is the screen that you will see to edit it:

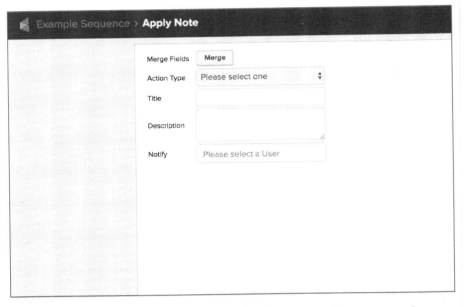

You can set a title and description, and even notify a user when the note is being created.

I like to apply notes to keep a dated history of actions that leads and clients have taken.

Create Task

Create Task gives you the ability to create to-do tasks for you or other Infusionsoft users on your account.
Tasks are extremely useful. They allow you to include nonautomated tasks like phone calls in your campaigns. Once a task is assigned, you can track when it is completed and by whom.

To use Create Task, add it to a sequence by dragging the icon onto the canvas. Open it up by double-clicking on it. This is what the screen would look like:

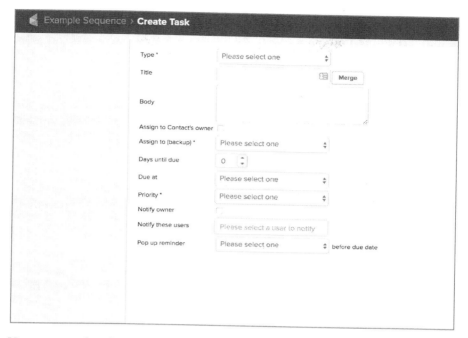

You can go back to the sequence by clicking the sequence name in the top left corner, and turn the task on by moving the toggle switch on the right from Draft to Ready.

Below that, you'll find that you can select the type, which is the type of task that you are assigning. The options for the types of tasks that you can assign are:

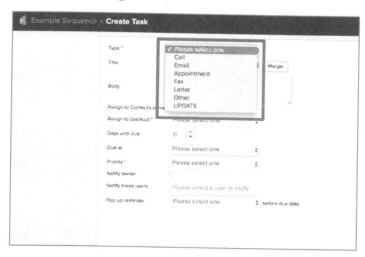

There are many different ways to use tasks. For example, you may want one of your staff to call a prospect after they've requested an appointment.

To set this up, first select the Type as Call. Next, write out the description of the task in the Title Section. You can also include further notes, including merge fields with the contact's info, in the body section. This way you or your staff won't have to waste time looking the information up before a call.

Below that, you have the option to Assign the task to the Contact's Owner. I will fully explain contact ownership in the next section. The gist is that each Contact Record can be assigned a contact owner, which is a user on your Infusionsoft account. This is a useful feature for companies that have more than one salesperson.

If you would like this task to be assigned to the contact owner (I'll explain how you set up a contact owner in the next section), then you can check that box. If you want to assign the task to a different user, then click the dropdown menu Assign To (backup) and choose a different user.

Days Until Due is not necessary; however, you can change the due date setting there. This will not impact when the task reminders are sent. Reminders are sent when the task is created. You can also change the due date time.

There are three options for priority: critical, essential, and nonessential. This changes the color of the flag associated with the task when you look at it in My Day, but otherwise doesn't do much. You must choose one to turn the task from Draft to Ready.

If you check the Notify Owner box, the task owner (either the Contact Owner or whomever else you assigned the task to) will get an email notification letting them know that they must complete the task. You can also notify other users by clicking their name in the Notify These Users section.

The pop-up reminder will send a pop-up reminder to the assigned Infusionsoft user at a set date/time before the due date of the task. This will pop up when somebody logs into his or her Infusionsoft account.

Personally, I find these pop-ups annoying; however, you might find them useful. I prefer using the My Day section of Infusionsoft instead, which I will go through in the last chapter of this book. It allows you to see all the tasks that have been assigned to you in one place.

Create Appointment

I don't typically use the Create Appointment process because, in order to use it, you need to use Infusionsoft's calendar, and most beginners don't use this, instead manually adding their appointments to their Outlook or Google calendars. As a beginner, you can ignore this feature and learn more about it once you have the basics down.

Set Field Value

You don't need to worry about this process. It's a more advanced feature and doesn't need to be used to get your first campaign up and running.

Assign an Owner

Assign an Owner allows you to assign a Contact to an Infusionsoft user (you or one of your staff) in your account. This is useful for businesses that have many sales staff or if you have different locations. Note: You can also change the owner of a Contact Record, even overriding old owners at certain stages of the sales/client process.
For instance, you may want a sales staff member to be the contact owner when someone is in the buying process and then have the contact change ownership once they have purchased.

Once you've added Assign an Owner to the Sequence Canvas and double-clicked to opened it, this menu comes up:

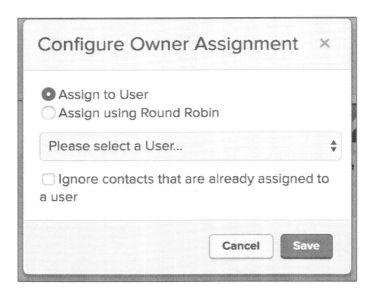

You have two options for assigning a contact to an owner. You can Assign to User or you can Assign Using Round Robin.

If you want every contact to be assigned to the same user, select Assign to User and choose the user that you want from the dropdown menu.

If you want to assign contacts to different users (like in the case of having multiple sales staff), use the Assign Using Round Robin.

When you select Assign Using Round Robin, you again will have two options. You can use the default setting, which means that each Infusionsoft user will get one Contact Record at a time until everyone has one. Then the cycle will start again so everyone gets an even number of Contact Records.

Or you can customize a Round Robin, which will assign the contacts based on your set users and ratios.

To set up a Custom Round Robin, you must first exit Campaign Builder. Next use the main dropdown menu in the top left corner and click Settings at the bottom of the CRM column.

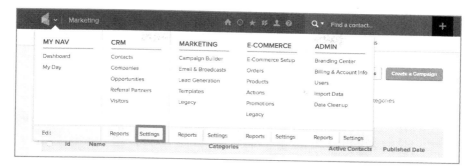

Once you open the Settings, select Round Robins from the options on the left side column.

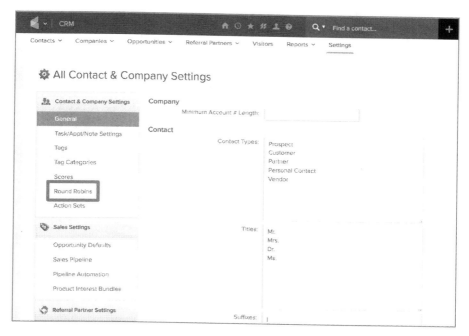

First, name your Round Robin. Next you can pick One Record Per Round (this will give all owners an even amount) or Distribute Records Based on Ratio.

For most businesses, it will make the most sense to use One Record Per Round.

This allows you to determine the number of Contact Records each user gets before moving onto the next user by setting it in the number section below:

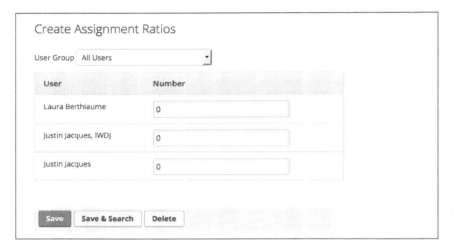

For example, if I want 'Laura Berthiaume' to get five Contact Records per round and 'Justin Jacques, IWDJ' to get only one record per round, I would change the numbers to 5 and 1. That would mean Laura would get five contacts assigned to her before Justin got one.

If you want everyone to get the same, you can just fill in 1 in the box for everyone.

Once you're done, click save, and you can go on back into your campaign to select that Round Robin.

Fulfillment List

Fulfillment List allows you to create a list (in the form of a .csv file) of contacts that have come through your campaign. This feature is useful if you need to export a list of contacts to be manually uploaded into another software. An example of this is if you want to send out physical mail from your office based on where contacts are in a campaign.
Here is what the Fulfillment List menu looks like:

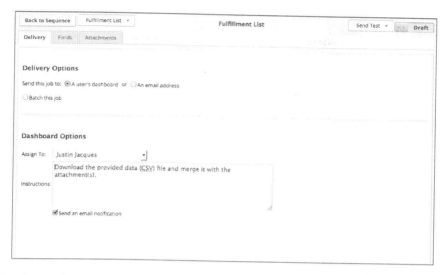

In the Delivery tab at the top (the default), your delivery options are to Send This Job To:

- **A user's dashboard:** That will go on to the assigned user's Infusionsoft dashboard when they log into Infusionsoft.

- **Email address:** This will send the fulfillment list to a specified email address.

Instead of having one fulfillment order for each contact that comes through the campaign, you can use Batch This Job. Using this setting will delay the creation of a fulfillment order. You can delay the fulfillment order either by waiting for a specified number of Contact Records or days.

Below that, you can also include instructions for the person who is assigned with this fulfillment.

If you click on the Fields tab at the top, you can include or remove any columns that will appear in the spreadsheet. This can make it easier to import into certain fulfillment programs because you can match up the titles in the CSV columns with the ones you need in the other program.

The Attachments tab (at the top) allows you to include any file attachments, including images or files that you have in

Infusionsoft. You can also upload a file and have that attach whenever the fulfillment list is created and sent.

Send HTTP Post

Send HTTP Post is a more advanced feature in Infusionsoft. It allows you to connect Infusionsoft to other software.
An example of outside software that you might want to use is Fix Your Funnel. Fix Your Funnel allows you to send physical mail (cards, postcards, brochures, etc.) and SMS messages to Contact Records. Go to http://justinjacques.com/amazing to get a list of some of my favorite third-party software for Infusionsoft.

Action Set (Legacy)

Action Sets are a legacy feature, meaning it's an old feature in Infusionsoft. It used to be a big part of the way that automation was set up in Infusionsoft but is not as useful anymore.
There are a few features of Actions Sets that can be useful; however, most of my clients do not use action steps.

At this point, it's not a beginner feature, so I'm not going to discuss it more here.

Other Processes

Start

The Start icon can be used when you want to start another chain of actions in the same sequence. For instance, you can't use multiple timers in the same chain, so you can start a new chain with a new start icon. If you wanted to send a confirmation email five minutes after someone booked an appointment, you would use a delay time. Then, if you wanted to send a reminder one day before the scheduled appointment, you could use a field timer with the Custom Field for your appointment as the trigger.

Notes

Notes allow you to leave notes in your sequence. This is useful because it allows you to include notes about how the campaign works or was set up (for yourself and other users that may come in to make changes/updates in the future).

Chapter 9: Segmenting Your List (to Make More Money) Using Decision Nodes

Decision Nodes are one of the most important features in Campaign Builder, but they are not found on the toolbar.

Decision Nodes allow you to put contacts through different sequences based on information in their record. For example, you may want to send older leads through a different promotion sequence than leads from the last thirty days. You can do this with decision nodes.

By segmenting your audience, even in just basic ways, you can speak to them more directly with more relevant communications.

Here is how you can use decision nodes in your campaigns.

First, we have a blank new campaign below:

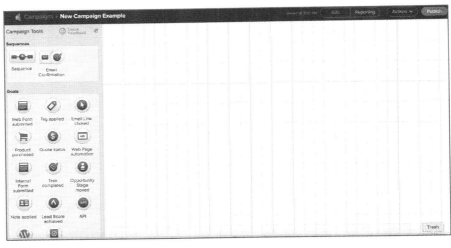

To start, you must have a goal to get people coming into this funnel, so let's use Sign Up for a Newsletter from a web form in this example.

This is now what the Campaign Canvas will look like:

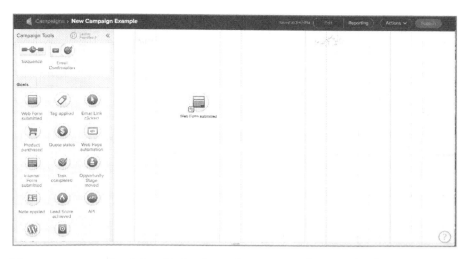

Next, you can double-clicked on the text underneath the icon to change it to 'Sign Up for a Newsletter'.

Next, you want to add a sequence to the Campaign Canvas.

Go to the Campaign Tools menu on the left and click and drag the sequence next to the Web Form icon. Double-click the text below the sequence to rename it from Untitled Sequence to Example Sequence 1.

Next, hover your cursor over the Sign Up for a Newsletter goal and you'll see a green arrow. Click on the green arrow and, while holding down the button on your mouse, drag it over to the new sequence. The sequence should then turn green or have a green box around it. When it's green, you can let go, and this will connect the goal to the sequence.

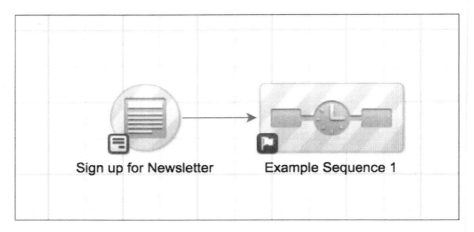

Now add a second sequence below the first sequence. Double-click below it to title it Example Sequence 2.

Again, hover over the Sign Up for a Newsletter icon. The green arrow will appear again. Click on that green arrow and hold and drag down to Example Sequence 2 to connect them. Once you have connected both sequences to the goal, a decision node will automatically appear that looks like this:

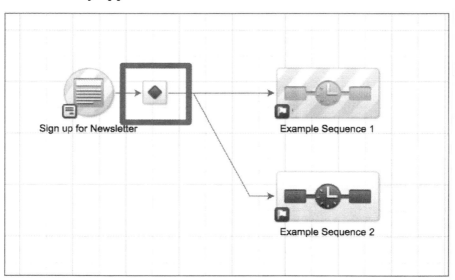

The Decision Node is the icon with the diamond in it. To set up the rules for the decision node, double-click on that icon.

This is the menu that will come up:

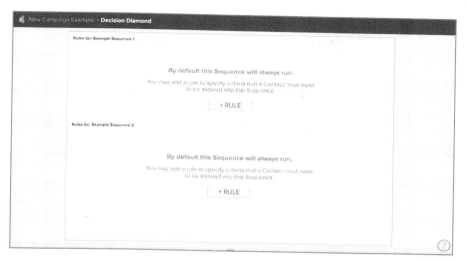

In order to pick a rule for a sequence, click on the + Rule button, and this menu will come up.

To edit the rule, click Please Select... to view a dropdown menu.

You can then click on **Contacts** from the dropdown menu.

This will cause a new Please Select... link to appear.

Click on the new Please Select... and you'll see a new dropdown menu. The options for this menu are Contact Fields, Appointment Info, Custom Fields, and Tags.

If you want to make a rule based on information in a Contact Record field, then choose Contact Fields. Now you can differentiate actions based on a Contact Record's city, birthday, job title, lead source, etc. You can see all the options here:

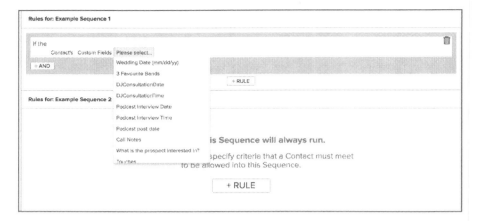

I'm going to use city in this example.

After you make a selection, the next option that you can select is shown below:

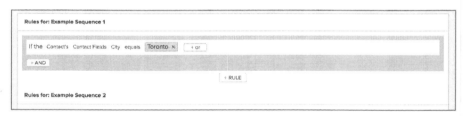

I'm going to choose Equals. After your selection, a box will appear where you can enter text. I wrote Toronto in this example.

If you hover over the rule, a **+ *Or*** button will appear. Clicking this will allow you a second text field for criteria (if you wanted to include two cities for this example).

Now all Contact Records in this campaign that have Toronto as their city will go to Example Sequence 1.

One important note about setting Rules is: if no rule is set, everyone who goes through the decision node will go through that sequence.

So, in our example, we must set a rule for Example Sequence 2, as shown below.

We want to make sure that any contact that has their city set as Toronto DOES NOT go through Example Sequence 2. We set that rule by selecting:

Contacts—Contact Field—City—then the difference is that we will select: does not equal. Then you type in Toronto, as seen below:

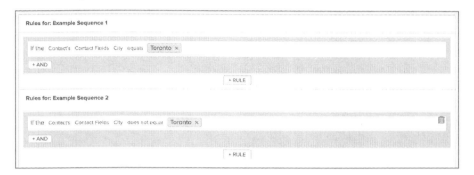

Decision nodes can be confusing when you first get started, but they are very powerful. I suggest trying something simple, like the example above, and then testing whether your rules are working by putting yourself through the campaign.

Chapter 10: How to Crush It with Infusionsoft: Campaign Builder Best Practices

Tip #1: Build Campaigns with Others in Mind

As you're building campaigns, remember that you may not be the only person using your Infusionsoft account. You may hire consultants or other staff who will go through and edit your campaigns.

When building campaigns, use notes and descriptive titles so that you can see what is going on when editing the campaign in the future or having other people edit it.

Here are the descriptions that should be in your campaigns:

i. Name the campaign after the purpose of the campaign.

ii. Name the action icons (emails, web forms, sequences) after their purpose in the campaign. For emails, I'll usually use my subject line as the email title.

iii. Make sure to include the URLs of landing pages used that are associated with each goals. For instance, what URL contains the web form in your Completed Web Form Goal. I've gone into campaigns and my client didn't know where the traffic was coming from because they did not do this.

Tip #2: Write Good Emails

There are three hard rules that I always tell my clients they must follow for email communication and follow-up. They'll help increase conversions and improve your relationships with your contacts.

RULE ONE: Know the Purpose

Always think about the purpose behind a campaign or email before you build it. Don't just send an email because you can. Have a purpose in mind for every campaign that you build and every email that you send.

Some of the reasons for reaching out to a Contact Record could be to build goodwill, make a sale, request information, or just to remind them of an upcoming event or appointment.

If you send too many emails that are irrelevant, you're going to train your audience to ignore your messages.

RULE TWO: Always Have a Call to Action

Your messages should always have a call to action. Explicitly tell your contact exactly what you want them to do, at least once in the communication.

You must also tell them exactly how to do it (e.g., go here, click this, fill in this form). It may seem like overkill to walk people through a process that seems so obvious, but it will increase your conversions.

A quick note is that your call to action doesn't always have to be a direct step toward buying. If you're sending useful information to your leads, the call to action might just be to ask your contact to reply with their experience. But you always want your clients to take some sort of action.

RULE THREE: Always Follow up with Leads at Least Three Times

Always follow up with leads at least three times. This means three follow-up messages after that initial request if they have not taken action.

People are busy and have very full inboxes. If it's an important and good message (see point 1), you are doing your customers or leads a favor by sending a follow-up email.

Tip #3: No Dead Thank-You Pages

Thank-you pages appear anytime someone completes an Infusionsoft form or completes a sale. You should never use the generic thank-you page template.

Instead of a generic thank-you page, you can:

- include another offer based on what they just purchased,

- ask a question in a survey to segment them,

- reinforce your brand (by sharing an article or video related to your business), or

- customize the thank-you experience with a video and make it feel like you put effort into it.

Tip #4: Do Not Manually Tag Your Contacts

Manual tagging is not a good practice. Over time, it's easy for you or your staff to forget which tags are supposed to go with which process. It's inevitable that something will get mixed up.

If you want to apply a tag to a contact to trigger follow-up after an offline activity—for instance, you had a sales call and the person isn't ready to buy—you could put them into a six-month follow-up sequence by applying a tag.

The best and most reliable way to do this is to use an internal form. You can then set it up to apply a tag once the form is completed, triggering the appropriate follow-up campaign.

Tip #5: Use a Double Opt-In

You may have noticed that some of your emails that are sent from Infusionsoft will end up in your Spam folder. The reason for this is likely because you have not used a double opt-in.

There are two main reasons for using a double opt-in:

1. Infusionsoft has two server farms that they send emails from. They send single opt-in emails from one group of servers and double opt-in emails from another server. In my experience, because of the server that the emails are coming from, the double opt-in emails are much more likely to end up in your client's inbox (instead of their spam).

2. Double opt-in is an industry best practice and will ensure that you do have permission to email your contacts.

You can add a double-opt-in to campaigns by adding the email confirmation sequence to the main Campaign Canvas in Campaign Builder. It will look like this:

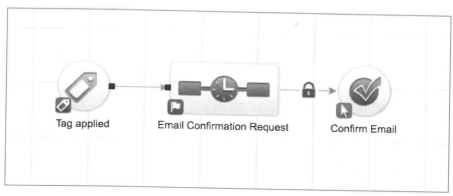

You are able to edit the confirmation email that is sent by clicking on the Email Confirmation Request Sequence. Note that you cannot edit certain parts of the email that must be there.

Tip #6: Copy Sequences and Parts of Campaigns Where Possible

Infusionsoft has a great feature that allows you to quickly copy and paste whole sequences or parts of sequences.

To copy and paste in a campaign, highlight the components that you want to copy (click, hold, and drag in the canvas area to create a box that includes all the elements you want to copy).

Now hold down the control button (on both Mac and PC). Next, left click your mouse on the elements (while holding the control button) and drag the elements to a blank spot on the Campaign Canvas.

This will then create a duplicate copy of whatever you highlighted. This can save you a ton of time, even if it's just small actions like timers, because you don't have to set them up multiple times.

Chapter 11: Avoid Accidentally Emailing 5,000 People and Then Awkwardly Apologizing...

How to Test Campaigns Before Launching Them

Ensuring that campaigns are set up properly before launching them is very important.

The first step is to review all emails and check for formatting and other errors. You can also check to see how the email looks in different browsers and mobile devices.

To do this, you can send a test email. Just go into the email editor (for each email) and click on the Send Test button in the top right corner.

The next step is to confirm that all your connections are set up in the right order. Review each action step, task, and tag to ensure it makes sense.

The best way to do this is to start the campaign with your own contact info and go through the sequence. This could mean applying the tag that triggers the campaign, completing the form, or performing whatever action that your contact would in order to go through the campaign.

Note: If a contact (or you, when testing) already has a tag that starts an unpublished campaign, they will not be put into a campaign when it is published. Only someone who has been tagged AFTER you have published the campaign will go through that campaign.

Expanding, Improving, and Maintaining: The Iterative Process

With Infusionsoft, it's best to just start building. Don't concern yourself with building the perfect campaign and thinking of every possible step on your first try. Build the best campaign that you can, then add on and make changes as using it shows you where improvements can be made.

Just like with any other form of marketing, the best results come from testing, not from creating the perfect marketing piece on the first try.

BE VERY CAREFUL ABOUT EDITING ACTIVE CAMPAIGNS

Here are two important notes about editing active campaigns:
1. If you add a new email to a sequence that has contacts in it, that email will be sent to anyone who has reached the end of that sequence in the last seven days. The email will even be sent if your contact is past the point that you edited in the sequence.

I know that this is confusing, so I'm going to try to make it easier by using an example.

You have a contact that is in a three-email reminder sequence and she received the last email three days ago without taking action, so she's still in that sequence. If you add a new email to that sequence and republish the campaign, she will get that email as soon as you hit publish.

Again, if she should have received that email in the last seven days, the email will be sent immediately.

2. If you add a new sequence to an active campaign, Infusionsoft will move any queued Contact Records into that new sequence. This could mean that you put contacts who haven't heard from you in years through your new sequence.

Queued contacts are contacts that have gone through all of the elements of a sequence, but did not achieve the final goal. When you click on the Reporting tab in a campaign, the gold/yellow number at the bottom of each sequence shows you how many contacts are queued in that sequence.

To avoid sending old (queued) contacts into the new sequence, I will show you how to remove those queued contacts from the sequence.

First, go to the campaign that you'd like edit. Click on the Reporting tab in the top right corner. Next select the Current option the Date Range Filter:

You will then see a layout of your campaign with a blue number at the top. That indicates the Contact Records that are currently going through the campaign (Active Contacts). The yellow number at the bottom indicates the Contact Records that are queued.

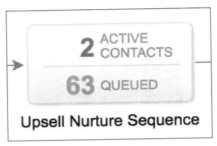

Upsell Nurture Sequence

If you're adding a sequence or onto a sequence that has the yellow/orange queued number, scroll over the sequence and a small icon with two people symbols will show up in the top right corner, like this:

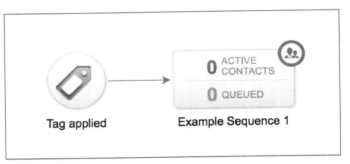

Tag applied   Example Sequence 1

Click on that icon to load the Active Contact Records in that sequence. Next, click the Edit Criteria/Columns button to see the queued Contact Records.

The following menu will load:

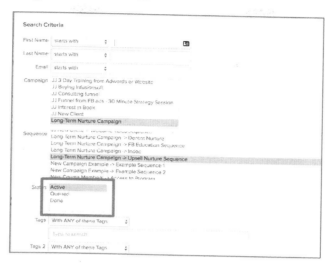

Scroll down and choose Status. The default selection for status will be active. Instead, change the status to queued.

Scroll down to the bottom and hit OK. This will load the list of queued Contact Records in that sequence. Next, click the Actions button at the top and the following menu will load:

Third from the bottom you'll see Start/Stop Campaign Sequence. Click on that and this is the page that will load:

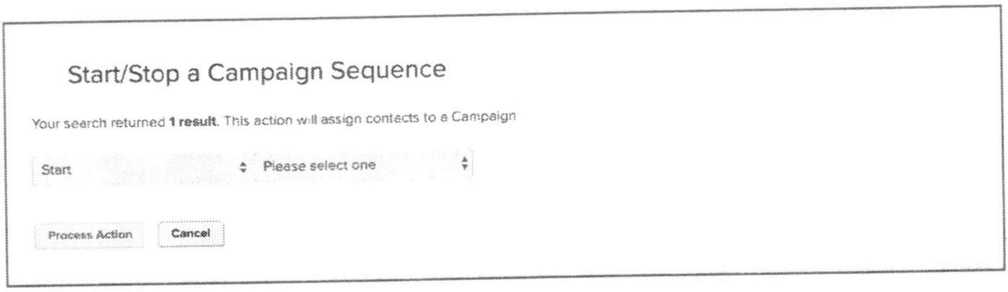

Start/Stop a Campaign Sequence

Your search returned **1 result**. This action will assign contacts to a Campaign

| Start | ⬍ | Please select one | ⬍ |

Process Action   Cancel

Click on the dropdown menu that says Start and select Stop.

On the next dropdown, select the name of your campaign that you want to stop. Once you've selected the name of the campaign, a third dropdown menu will appear to the right.

From the third dropdown, select the name of the sequence that you want to remove your contacts from.

Note: This is why it's also good to be descriptive in your titles. You won't have to guess at the campaign or sequence name when you see a list of them together.

Once you've selected the correct sequence, press Process Action to remove all queued Contact Records from your sequence. You can now add on additional sequences without worrying about sending out emails to Contact Records who should not receive them.

Chapter 12: Increase Email Deliverability and Manage Your Contacts in Infusionsoft

Where Are Your Contacts?

To find your contacts, click on the main navigation arrow at the top left.

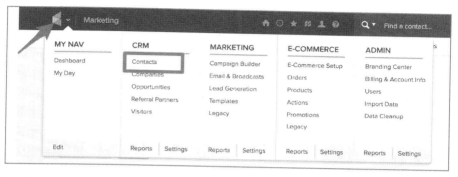

In the CRM column, click on the list titled Contacts.

Now your list of contacts will load.

How to Use the Contacts Area

When you first go into the Contacts Area, you'll either see some of your contacts (if you did a previous search, first image below) or the search criteria if this is your first time searching for contacts. If you see a list of contacts and you want to get your full list, hit the New Search button (as shown below):

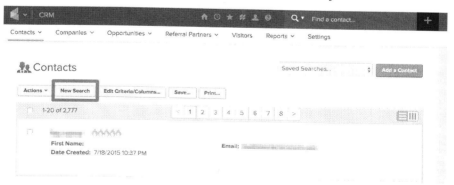

You will then see this screen (your app may have opened this screen up to start):

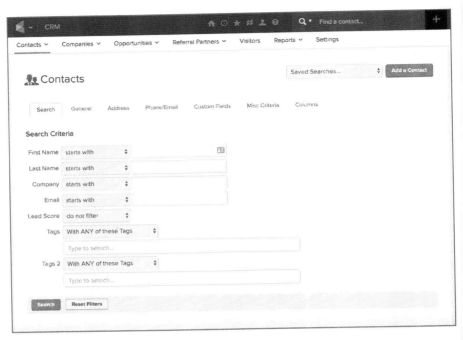

By hitting the Start Over button, you are clearing the previous search that you preformed. If you want to see all of your contacts in a list, just scroll down to the bottom of the page and hit the Reset Filters button.

Once the filters have been reset and the page reloads, scroll down and hit the Search button. Your full list of contacts will then load on the next page.

Generally, a full list of your contacts isn't going to be very useful, so I'll show you how to get more out of the search function.

First, go back into the search section by clicking on the New Search button:

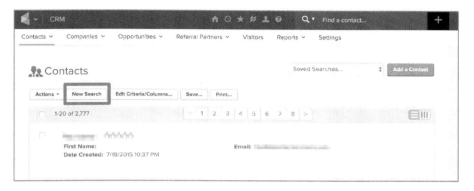

Once the screen loads, you will see tabs at the top that include Search, General, Address, Phone/Email, Misc. Criteria, and Columns.

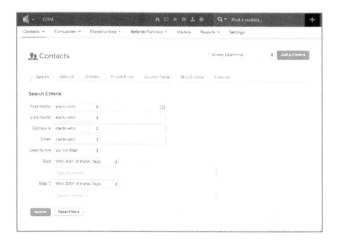

I'll take you through each of these and show you a couple of examples of useful searches.

In the search tab, you have the ability to search by first or last name, company, and email. These are the general searches that can be useful if you are looking for a specific person.

Below those options is Lead Score, which a more advanced feature of Infusionsoft. It will not be covered in this book.

Tag searches are the next option, and these are very useful. You can search your records for people who have or do not have a specific tag.

For example, you could search for people who have purchased Product A but not Product B, as long as you were applying tags to people based on purchases.

To search by tags, scroll down to the Tag IDs field option. Next, select "With ANY of these Tags" from the dropdown menu and select the tag you want to use. For this example, you would select the Purchase Product A tag.

Below that, for Tags 2, you would use the dropdown to select "Doesn't have ANY of these tags." Then select the "Purchased Product B" tag in the box beneath the dropdown.

When you hit search, all of the contacts that have purchased Product A but not purchased Product B will be displayed.

I find the tag search to be the most powerful part of contact search. You can click through the other tabs to see what other fields you can perform searches by.

How to Get Your Current Contacts into Infusionsoft

In this section, I'm going to go through the few ways that you can add and organize contacts in Infusionsoft to ensure that everyone is in the right place.

List Import

To import a list of contacts into Infusionsoft, go to the main menu dropdown bar and under the admin column you'll find Import Data, as seen below:

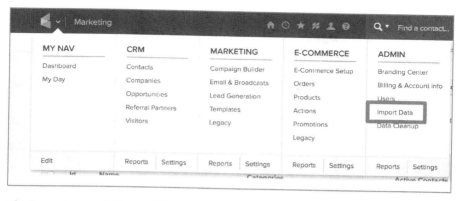

Click on Import Data. This will bring up the menu below, the Import Data Into Infusionsoft menu:

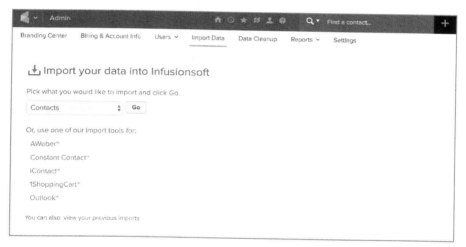

On this page you can import Contact Records, companies, or tags. You can also use an import tool to automatically import contacts from five different companies: AWeber, Constant Contact, iContact, 1ShoppingCart, and Outlook.

If you're not importing from any of those five software products, you can just use the default import by selecting Contacts on the dropdown menu at the top of the page and then hitting Go. Once you hit Go, you will see this menu or this page:

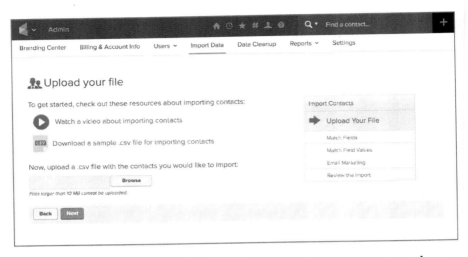

Next, download the sample CSV file and paste your contact data into the appropriate title tops of the sample CSV file. In the sample CSV file, you will see the following column titles:

- Firstname
- Middlename
- Lastname
- Title
- Suffix
- Company
- Lead source
- Job title
- Contact notes
- Tags

Fill in all of these columns by matching up your data with the appropriate column title. There are additional notes in the CSV for how to fill it out properly. For example, with the tag column, multiple tags can be entered; they just have to be separated by a comma.

Next, save that CSV file with your data. Then upload that file by hitting the Browse button, finding the file on your computer, and hitting the Next button.

You'll be brought to a page where you're able to match the titles at the top of the CSV file to an Infusionsoft field. You're also able to add custom fields or create tags from your field values.

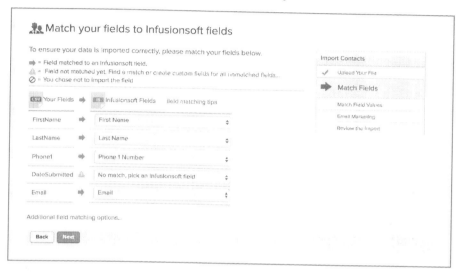

Make sure that the fields from your CSV file are properly matched up with the field names in Infusionsoft.

Infusionsoft is pretty good at matching, but you will want to go through and make sure that the values are correct. Once you've matched the values, hit Next.

One of the last steps is confirming whether or not you plan on email marketing to these contacts. That menu looks like this:

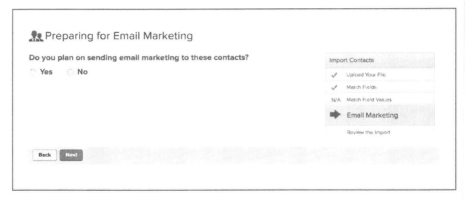

If you click no, you will not be able to email these contacts.

If you click yes, you'll then have to fill out a questionnaire about how you got these contacts. The reason that Infusionsoft does this is to prevent their customers from sending out spam from harvested lists. Infusionsoft is very picky about who they allow you to email because, if their users send out too many emails that are marked as spam, all of their users' email delivery rates will go down.

Below is the questionnaire:

Preparing for Email Marketing

Do you plan on sending email marketing to these contacts?

○ Yes   ○ No

How did these contacts sign up for your marketing?

○ Filled out a Web Form on my website

○ Purchased a product from me

○ Attended an Event

○ Personal Interaction (Business Card, Phone Call, Email, LinkedIn)

○ Social Media

○ Through an Association/Membership

○ Through and Affiliate/JV Partner

○ Through a third party (Purchased List)

Which service provider(s) have you been sending this list through?

○ None
○ Aweber
○ Constant Contact
○ Mail Chimp
○ 1 Shopping Cart
○ Other

What method(s) of opt-in have you been using?

○ Single Opt In
○ Double Opt In

Import Contacts

✓ Upload Your File

✓ Match Fields

N/A Match Field Values

➡ Email Marketing

Review the Import

Be truthful with your answers in the questionnaire. If you do send out spam, your account can be closed and banned. Again, Infusionsoft is very serious about ensuring that their users are only sending email to people who have agreed to receive their email.

Once you've completed the survey, the last step is to review the import. You'll be able to see each contact record. Scroll through it to ensure that all the information is lined up properly. When you're done, scroll down to the bottom and hit Done. All of those contact records will be added to your account.

Adding and Editing Custom Fields

By using Custom Fields, you're able to add extra data to Contact Records beyond the default fields in Infusionsoft. For example, you might want to include the day that a Contact Record first became a customer so you can send out an anniversary card.

To add a Custom Field, go to the top main menu under the Admin column and click on the Settings button at the bottom.

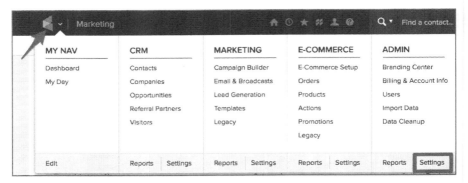

The screen below will load. At the top of this screen, you will see the title Custom Fields, and right below that you'll see "Set Up Custom Fields For." To create or edit your custom fields, hit Go.

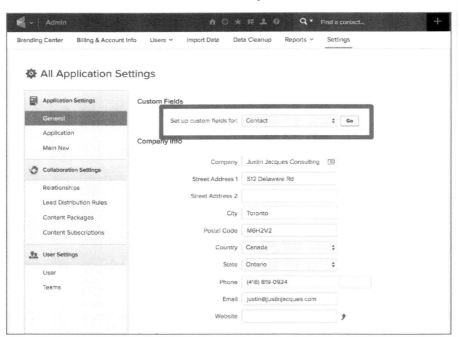

This will bring you to a new screen that lists your Custom Fields. At the top of the page, you will see a dropdown menu where you can choose Field, Tab, or Header.

Select Field and hit Add.

Now you can add a Name for your Custom Field and choose the type of field. Using the example above, you can label the field "Customer Acquisition Date."

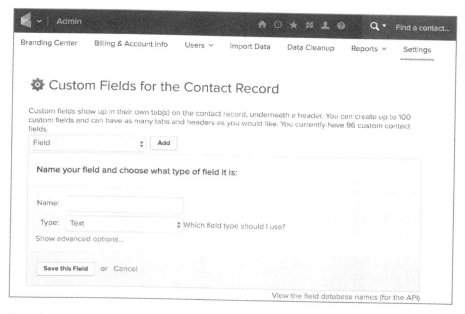

For the dropdown menu Type, you have a long list of options, shown here:

The Type is important because it'll ensure that your data is properly stored. In this case, we want to select Date as our field because it will make the field a calendar date. Once you've selected the type of field, you can hit Save This Field.

Note that you are only allowed to have one hundred Custom Fields on your account. This may seem like a lot; however, I've had numerous customers who have used them all. Later on, they couldn't do what they wanted because they had no custom fields left.

If you would like to edit a previously made custom field, scroll over the field that you want to edit. A pencil and a trashcan icon will appear. Click on the pencil icon to edit the field or the trashcan to delete the field.

Chapter 13: Newsletters, Templates, Branding, and Other Core Infusionsoft Functions

Email Broadcasts

Email broadcasts allow you to send out a one-time email to all or part of your list.

This is great for sending out email newsletters or one-time promotional emails. If you are building out a promotion with multiple follow-up steps or messages, I would suggest that you build that in Campaign Builder instead.

To send an Email Broadcast, go to the main navigation menu in the top left corner. Under the Marketing column, click on Email & Broadcasts

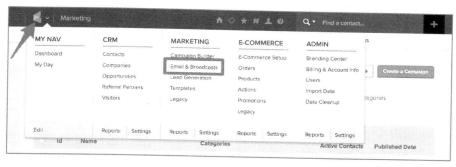

and you'll open up a page that looks like this:

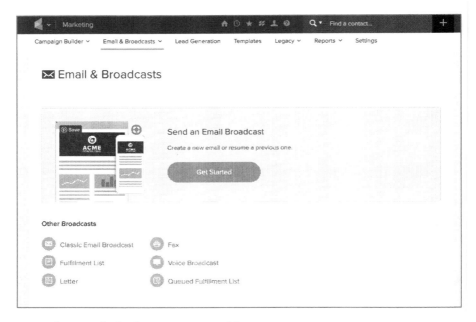

From here, click the Get Started button.

This will bring you to a page that looks similar to the email builder:

Start by choosing the template you want to use by scrolling over it and clicking on "Use Template."

Once you're in the email builder, you also have the option to save it as a template, making it easier to send out a similar broadcast in the future.

At the top of the previous screen, you would click on the My Templates link in the header to bring up your templates.

Desiging the email is the same as setting up a Campaign Builder email, so I will not review it again here.

At the top, you can change whom the email will be coming from by clicking on the pencil next to From.

You can choose between the Contact Record's Owner and any of the account users, or you can enter any email address you'd like by selecting "Other..."

Note that the Contact's Owner will come from that Contact Record's owner, which could be different for different contacts depending on how you've assigned the Contact Records.

Below that, you can select the recipients whom the email will go to. You can use either a group of people with a specific tag or do a saved search of the contacts.

If you want to send the email to a group of people with a specific tag or tags, all you have to do is search for them right in that recipient bar and hit enter when you find the right ones.

If you want to do a search, just click the New Search link right below the recipient field. This is the exact same contact record search that was in the last section. You can find contacts with any of the criteria in their record—location, tags, custom fields, purchases, etc.

When you select the criteria you want, just hit the Search button and they'll automatically get added to the recipient bar.

On the top right, you will find the buttons to preview or test this email.

I highly suggest testing the email before sending it out to hundreds or thousands of people.

Once you've determined the list of recipients, hit the Review and Send button where you can schedule the email to be sent out or send it out immediately.

If everything looks good and all the settings are correct, you can hit the Send/Schedule button.

If at any point you want to leave and finish the broadcast later, you can hit the exit button in the top right corner and it will autosave to your drafts.

Your drafts are available on this screen, the same screen as your templates, in the top menu:

Templates & Branding

In Infusionsoft, you can create reusable templates for emails, web forms, landing pages, and letters. In order to do this, open up the main menu in the top left corner, and click Branding Center under the Admin column.

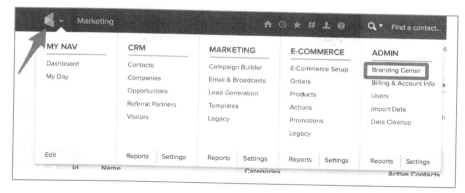

You will then see this menu:

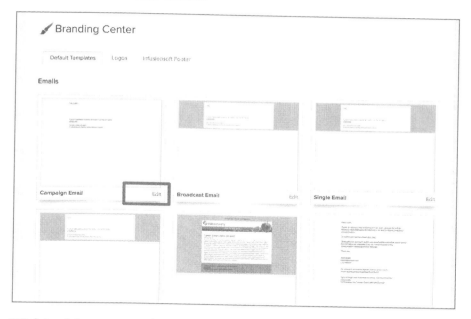

Within this area, you're able to edit templates for emails, web forms, landing page, letters, and order form/thank-you pages.

Most of the email templates are for the old email builder and are not mobile-friendly, so don't worry about editing these.

You can change the look of the confirmation email here, but note that you still can't change the language in the bottom section. This is fixed so that it complies with anti-spam laws.

The next tab in the Branding Center is Logos. This is where you can add your business logo, which is automatically added to certain elements throughout Infusionsoft.

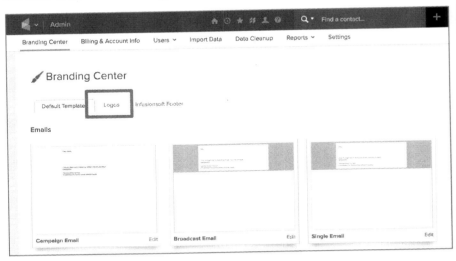

To do this, click on the Logos tab, next to the Default Template tab. On the new screen, you'll see Default Logo and Logo Locations. Here you can upload any logos that you have.

To add a new image, click Edit on the Default logo. When the new window pops up, click the Add New Image button, and then you'll be able to upload any file. Select the file from your computer and hit Open. That will add the image onto your screen. Finally, click Save. This will add the new default logo and will allow you to use that logo in other communications on your Infusionsoft account.

Turning Off the Infusionsoft Logo in Your Email

The last tab in the Branding Center is for the Infusionsoft logo.

I recommend removing the Infusionsoft logo because it is a distraction from your marketing message.

Note: Infusionsoft will pay you a referral fee if you leave the link in your footer and someone clicks it and ends up buying the software. For most businesses, I don't think that the referral fee is worth taking away from their own marketing message.

If you want to turn off the "Powered by Infusionsoft," click on the Infusionsoft Footer tab and scroll down to the bottom.

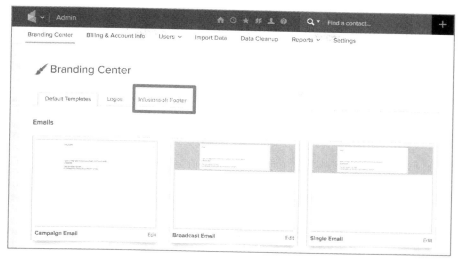

You'll see Settings and "Allow Infusionsoft footer in emails." Switch that to No. You'll also see "Allow Infusionsoft footer to link to Infusionsoft." Also switch that to No.

Once you've changed the settings, hit the Save button in the bottom right.

Users

Users are people who are going to be working in your Infusionsoft account. Depending on the package that you have, you will have a different number of users that you're allowed. The number increases with the size of the package, and you can also add on additional user licenses for a monthly fee.

To add or edit your users, go to the main menu and click the Users button under the Admin column, as seen below:

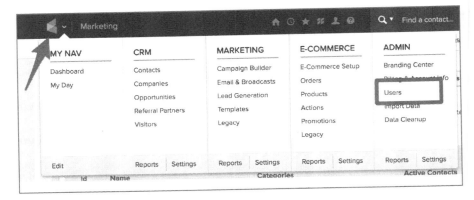

This will show your list of users:

To add a new user, click the Add Users button. You can then put in the name and email address of the new user that you want to use.

E-Commerce

E-Commerce is not a beginner concept in Infusionsoft. I believe knowing how to use Campaign Builder and building your first funnel is the first step, so e-commerce will not be covered in this book. However, if you do need help with your e-commerce, feel free to go here: http://justinjacques.com/apply-for-strategy-session/ to apply for a free one-hour strategy session.

Get Three Bonuses That Will Help You Create Your Core Infusionsoft Sales Funnel in Seven Days

Get $359 worth of amazing info and tools that will help you plan, implement, and optimize your core sales funnel in seven days—instead of months or years.

...from prospect to lead to one-time buyer **to multi-buyer**.

Remember, amateur marketers make one offer and call it a day when they get a sale. Pro marketers keep making offers. If you're not already doing that, get the bundle to see how you can make it work for your business.

Get it here now >> http://justinjacques.com/amazing/

What You Get in the Beginner's Bonus Bundle:

- My Core Sales Funnel Blueprint with step-by-step instructions to the five parts of a core sales funnel that maximizes profit for each lead.

- My Campaign Visualizer so you can plan and build your funnel easily without the tech stuff, just a basic mind map of how your sales funnel/processes should go.

- My guide to the Nine Best Infusionsoft Add-Ons to do even more with Infusionsoft, like send welcome gifts, direct mail, schedule appointments automatically, and connect your PPC to Infusionsoft seamlessly.

Click here to get your Beginner's Bonus Bundle

If you want to finally figure out Infusionsoft and get your core sales funnel running in the next week, you MUST take me up on this offer.

Note: This offer is only available to readers of this book, so please do not share the link.

Ready to go from no Infusionsoft knowledge to having the software rock your business in the next seven days?

If yes, you have two options:

1. You can go to this website:
   http://justinjacques.com/amazing